"I have known Sherife for man_____ ____ ...ave witnessed his special gift for teaching and developing others. In this book, Sherife articulates an honest approach to seeing the world and our place in it. He shares a practical vision for living that can help us navigate the ups and downs of life and unlock our full potential, allowing us to thrive. This book provides a vital blueprint for anyone who wants to get unstuck and take their life to new heights."

— **Stu Schmill**

# SUPER VISION

# SUPER VISION

## AN EYE-OPENING
## APPROACH TO
## GETTING UNSTUCK

**Sherife AbdelMessih**

R

RINASCENTE

NEW YORK

Published in the United States in 2023
First Edition
2nd Printing

R
Rinascente
New York

ISBN 979-8-9879606-1-5 (paperback)
ISBN 979-8-9879606-0-8 (ebook)

*To Yousriya…*

# CONTENTS

## Part III: The Road Less Traveled

# PREFACE

When I look back at the kind of education I received in school, and the type that billions of students continue to receive today, I can't help but think about how those critical young years are wasted on teaching material that is easy to read and rarely used in the real world. How we were tossed into the real world completely unprepared for the political battles at work and the two-faced nature of many people. How we were never formally taught crucial skills, such as how to set boundaries with the people closest to us or how to choose lovers.

It is no surprise that the larger population on our planet today is mostly unhappy with the lives that they lead. We spent very little time in our formal education getting acquainted with the tools and pathways that give meaning and happiness in life, the frameworks that lead to inner peace and contentment. Our education didn't even include the best practices that lead to focus and inspiration and how to ultimately unleash our creative powers and leave our mark on the world. All such skills were banished to the self-help corner of the local bookstore or library.

Instead it was more important in school to spend a dozen years learning about geography, social studies, and literature. With all the respect I have for these disciplines, I find it impossible to see how an education can be complete without a solid and grounding education in life skills. That is why most of us remain illiterate to this day when it comes to matters of emotional intelligence, social intelligence, how to be happy, how to achieve our dreams, and how to select the right dreams in the first place.

I am happy with what I have experienced and accomplished in life so far. I was fortunate to achieve and experience many things way ahead of my age. To be a pioneer in several fields ahead of my time. Yet when I look back, I recall so many instances where I needed to get out of my own way. I wasn't aware that I was my biggest enemy. Simply because such life skills are not taught in school or even the workplace. But they should be, for they have the power to produce leaders that are more enlightened, more compassionate, more happy, and ultimately more healthy for themselves, their families, and everyone else they interact with on a daily basis.

I only learned these lessons late in my career—either from lots of trial and error or by magically stumbling on the right philosophy. But I can only imagine how my life would have been different had I learned these lessons earlier. So I write this book with the intention to share these valuable lessons with you to help you grasp the life you have been looking for but seems to have been eluding you. Or possibly to grasp the life you never realized could exist and could be yours. Learning is a never-ending process. I am only a master of my craft because I am a lifetime student.

In all cases, I hope that after you finish reading this book you will see yourself and the world around you differently. And you will realize the immense power you have within you to change any situation you find yourself in and ultimately to change your life and possibly the lives of those around you as well.

# FIRST INTRODUCTION

Happiness has become the world's most sought-after drug. Everyone is either looking for it or wants more of it. Happiness is an emotional state characterized by contentment in addition to other pleasurable feelings such as joy. Most people experience happiness for a short period of time, only to have this state of mind robbed from them by external or internal events.

As we will learn in this book, when we lose this state of happiness it is actually us who rob ourselves of it. We alone have the power to give ourselves happiness or take it away. In this book we will learn how to develop a new lens of seeing the world around us, our lives, and the events that unfold in it. In addition, we will develop new muscles that help us control how we react to such events. These muscles and this new lens will transform the way in which we experience our life and how we feel about it—without anything needing to change in our environment. We will learn that when we are happy, we are not happy *because*, rather we are happy *despite*.

# SECOND INTRODUCTION

Seventy percent of the 375 million sensory receptors in the human body are used for vision. While nearly half of the brain's known resources are involved in vision. The overwhelming emphasis on vision in our biology sends us a clear message: What you see and how you see is more vital than any other activity you do. It determines every other activity in your life. If you don't get the first part accurate, you are bound to struggle in other areas of your life. And that is certainly why we struggle, or suffer.

As humans, we like to take matters into our own hands. Many of us are always taking action. We use our hands and legs to go after what we want, to clear anything in our way. We pursue our dreams, attack our goals, defend our rights. When we don't get the results we want, we take action again, perhaps trying a different course.

There is one thing we don't realize. What if we can't get the results we want because our vision has been compromised? What if we can't perceive things properly? What if our sight is leading us to a state where we are not chasing our goal, but something that looks a lot like it? What if our values and rights were not threatened, and we were expending so much valuable time and energy in defending them?

In *Super Vision*, we learn about all our short circuits that have been causing us to not see properly and consequently go off track. We'll learn to see the world and ourselves with a sharper lens that allows us to live happier and more impactful lives. We'll encounter multiple frameworks to help us improve how we see ourselves and the world around us, and how we perceive events taking place in our lives, empowering us to struggle less, and advance and rejoice more.

# PART I

## WHAT THEY DIDN'T TEACH YOU

# 1

# THOU SHALL NOT EXPECT

*Blessed is he who expects nothing,*
*for he shall never be disappointed.*
— Alexander Pope

You have been here before. Several times actually, too many to count. You have been disappointed so many times in your life that you have gotten tired of it. You wonder why it has become so difficult for your simple and rational expectations to materialize. You are not asking for much, you expect the bare minimum from others, the normal, yet you continue to be disappointed. Given the large number of interactions we have with people on a daily basis, at work, in our personal lives, running random errands, there are so many opportunities to be disappointed and it seems that we catch them all.

What if I told you there's a way for you to never be disappointed again? What if I told you that you were actually disappointing yourself all along? You were doing it by setting expectations for everything, by having a clear picture of how certain events completely beyond your control should unfold, and by getting upset when they don't conform to your expectations.

You might be a bit puzzled, thinking that your expectations are not unreasonable, that they lay out how an experience should unfold in any normal scenario. Yet you forget that the word "normal" is actually something very individual that can change based on culture, values, and upbringing. You also forget that most people are not necessarily rational when it comes to their behavior.

Having expectations for how people are going to behave or how certain situations are going to unfold is like having expectations for what direction the wind is going to blow or how much rain is going to pour from the sky. Both are beyond your control, so when you create expectations for them you are simply setting yourself up for disappointment. Instead, when you don't have any expectations, everything becomes what it *is* instead of what it was *supposed to be*. It simply becomes a very rainy day as opposed to a day that should have been sunny. It becomes a rude cashier at the supermarket as opposed to one who was supposed to be polite.

When you have no expectations, your mind is ready to accept and process any reality you encounter for what it is as opposed to feeling like it was knocked off course by an anomaly; something that was not supposed to happen, something that doesn't make any sense. When your mind expects things to turn out a certain way only to find the events taking a different, less pleasing direction, it becomes confused. Your brain does not like to be wrong. Whenever your mind has to second-guess the assumptions it made in order to form a certain expectation, it becomes a very painful process, and that is why you feel bad. In such situations, it is like your brain has to second-guess everything it knows about life and question what other things might not be true as well. Biologically, psychologically, and philosophically, expectations lead to disappointments.

When someone makes a promise to you, do not expect them to keep it. If they end up keeping it, you will be happy, and if they don't, you won't be upset or disappointed because you were not holding them to any bar. If you have a new or old friend who has been very good to you, do not expect them to always stay like that. If one day they suddenly turn on you or behave in an awkward way that you can't explain, you won't be tormented by it because you had no expectation of them to conform to your idea of what "normal" behavior should be like. If you did a lot of favors for one of your colleagues at work, if you were the reason why they kept their job and didn't get fired, don't expect them to repay you. In fact, don't raise your level of expectation of them by an inch relative to anyone you just met. Otherwise you are holding them to a bar that they might not be able to live up to, and the only person who will suffer if that happens is you.

Understand that human nature is forgetful, ungrateful, and perhaps weak as well. Someone will break from character at some point. If you had expectations, you will be disappointed. If you didn't have expectations, it will be nothing more to you than what simply happened. Someone broke from character, too bad for them, but there was no negative effect on you emotionally.

I am not asking you to be suspicious of everyone around you and to expect that they will all disappoint you. That is an expectation of its own, except that it is a negative expectation. I don't want you to have any expectations at all, either positive or negative, when it comes to events and the people around you because you cannot control them. All you need to do is to simply be aware of all the possibilities that could unfold around you so that you can be in a position where you are able to maneuver and protect yourself accordingly from any situation that unfolds. Do not let your guard down too low because you assumed a certain environment was safe. You might realize otherwise when it is too late.

What does life look like when you have no expectations of anyone or anything? There are very few bad surprises, no disappointments, and you are rarely caught off guard. If anyone inflicts malice on you, intending to hurt you, it actually does not sting as much because you are open to all possibilities unfolding in your life. You don't necessarily have to imagine every single scenario in advance, but in every scenario that unfolds, you are happy to quickly integrate each scenario into your visual database as another possibility that could have happened, regardless of how unlikely it might have been or how little sense it makes.

It makes little sense why people disappoint you, because humans are emotional creatures not rational ones. Our actions are driven by feelings not logic. Most humans will rarely do what is good for you, let alone what is good for themselves because they are not able to perceive situations and process them properly. People who regularly behave logically are a rare specimen of the human species. They are people who were able to reach an advanced level of mastering their emotions and controlling their behavior, and we should view them as the exception, not the rule. People are bound to make mistakes over and over again. It does not mean that they have anything against you or that you are a direct target. It is mostly self-sabotage on their part, so don't get involved in their behavior by taking it personally.

When you learn to have no expectations of people, you will have far fewer interruptions to your day because you will simply carry on when an unusual event unfolds instead of stopping in shock and taking the rest of the day or week to try and understand what happened and recover from it. You will find it is much easier to focus on your journey and easier to generate results and progress. You will feel more healthy and will simply smile on your misfortunes the same way you smile on your fortunes. After you master this skill, you will be surprised how much energy was previously wasted on such disappointments that you inflicted on yourself. So much energy is sucked out of you, so many bad moods triggered as a result of your own making, setting expectations that were bound to lead to disappointments.

Next time you feel bad, ask yourself, was this because of an expectation that was not met? If yes, immediately realize that it was of your own doing, and you can feel good again as quickly as you can let go of the expectation that you never should have had in the first place.

# 2

# THINK NEGATIVELY

*Whoever cannot seek the unforeseen sees nothing.*
*For the known way is an impasse.*
— Heraclitus

Negativity is not always a bad thing. Testing negative for a disease is certainly not bad. In this chapter, we'll explore another powerful instance where being negative can be a very useful thing.

You have been taught to think positively, to be optimistic, to look at all the upsides. That can serve as a good motivator to push you into pursuing a task or a project that you have been wanting to do for a while. But that is only half of the binoculars you need to succeed. Without thinking deeply about all of the things that could go wrong, you might be dooming yourself to fail badly and to hurt yourself before you even get started. We were taught to be positive, to expect the best. But what if that's partly why we keep stumbling and tripping over ourselves? When you are always thinking about the best that could come, you fail to foresee the bad that is waiting around the corner, and if you can't see the bad then you can't avoid it.

When we embark on a mission or engage with a person, we usually do so because we expect it will result in some gain or benefit on our part. Because we are motivated by the gain, it is easy for us to be blindsided by all the potential outcomes that could go wrong. When we go into something expecting good to come out, only to find insult and injury as the result, we become almost traumatized by the experience. Such trauma comes into effect because we did not anticipate that the result of engaging in this activity or interaction with that person could end so badly. It is as if our brain is reacting to its failure to predict an outcome by inflicting pain on itself as a punishment.

This circuit failure can be prevented if we learn to think about and anticipate all the things that could go wrong from the actions we undertake and the people we interact with in advance, instead of just thinking about the positive upside that motivated us to take this action. This applies to the big things in our life as well as the little things, such as greeting someone with good morning and expecting a cheerful good morning back, only to encounter their grumpy facial expression and no verbal response as they walk by. Anticipating that people might not return our polite gestures takes away the element of surprise and the shock and pain that might come with it.

It also applies to the big things in life, such as anticipating that the project we are embarking on and are about to pour our whole life into might run out of money and we might have to abort it halfway through. This is the opposite of the naive positive perspective which makes us think that just because we are embarking on something noble, positive, and selfless it cannot fail because we are doing something good for the world.

The power of anticipation and thinking of all the negative outcomes that could result in a situation has been used by generals for thousands of years on the battlefield. The most victorious generals do not rush onto the battlefield beating their chest and flaunting their large army behind them. The reason victory is a trend on their résumé is because they sit down before they take any action and calculate what could go wrong and create ways to deal with those situations should they happen. What if the enemy attacks our flank instead of attacking us head-on as we expect them to? What if our spies turn out to be wrong about the size of the enemy's army—and what if it's larger? What if the weather turns out to be horrible and it pours rain as the battle wages?

The point of this exercise is not to scare you with everything that could go wrong and demoralize you from taking action. On the contrary, it is meant to help you succeed better by forcing you to prepare in advance for scenarios you might not have realized you would face. The more prepared you are, the more likely you are to succeed. Moreover, there is a big difference between an army that has lost a battle yet is still strong enough to retreat and maneuver in order to fight another day and an army whose morale has been completely obliterated, which makes it almost impossible for any general to regroup his soldiers to fight another day. There is nothing that can destroy the morale of a person or a team more than an event that was guaranteed to be a success only to result in complete failure. This is ultimately what you are setting yourself up for when you do not leverage the power of anticipation.

The power of anticipation is evident if we look at a sport like boxing. Any experienced boxer will tell you that it is not the biggest punch that knocks you out. It is the one that you didn't see coming. You could stand in the ring and take very powerful blows that have little effect on you because they are coming head-on and you can see them coming. But one punch with only a fraction of the force could pummel you flat on the floor because it came out of nowhere, it penetrated your defenses, it seems to hurt mentally even more than physically because it paralyzed your brain for a second. In boxing that is a second too long.

On the other hand, when you see a punch coming, your body braces for the impact. Your neck muscles contract in order to provide better support for your head that is about to receive the blow. Your brain gives you a heads up that this is about to hurt. You have been put on full alert and are prepared for the force that is coming. This preparation, or lack thereof, is also why we can be knocked down much more easily when we fail to see a punch coming, in boxing or in real life. But why would we not learn to anticipate the negative things that could happen so that we can be prepared for them mentally and practically?

Sometimes our wishful thinking, naivete, or even ego gets in the way and tells us that nothing bad can happen. We won't have an accident, we won't run out of money, we won't be cheated on, when in fact, all indicators are pointing to that as the most likely outcome. Sometimes we don't see it because we refuse to see it, we don't want to see it, we cannot bear the thought of that negative reality, so we refuse to admit to ourselves that it is a possibility, let alone prepare for it.

That is why you have to leverage the power of anticipation. You have to anticipate in every important situation that something could go wrong. That way, if it does, you rob the bad outcome of its power to knock you down. Because you already anticipated it. This anticipation doesn't mean that you should be pessimistic. Just realistic.

Humans are wishful thinkers by nature, so we refuse to see how things could take an unexpected turn. Such a simple technique can save you a great deal of time, pain, and money. Even if you don't manage to slip the punch, it will feel more like a mosquito bite instead of a sledgehammer because it was not a total surprise.

We can incorporate this framework into our professional lives by taking the time to anticipate all the things that could go wrong before we enter a meeting or embark on a project. Before going into a job interview, think about what you would do if you encountered a rude interviewer. Will you walk out or push through without compromising your dignity? When you have time to think it through in advance, you are able to make the right decision when faced with this situation as opposed to going with whatever your reflexes force on you in the heat of the moment.

This applies to your personal life as well. Before going into a new relationship, realize that this person could cheat on you, or they could suddenly stop talking to you and ghost you. Beyond the practical considerations of how you would deal with that, it greatly cushions the blow and the damage that is inflicted on you if it happens because you already foresaw this as a theoretical possibility—as opposed to having your reality shattered and being caught off guard because you couldn't even imagine that such a person could be capable of doing this to you.

Many times when we suffer from a bad event, the damage we do to ourselves is far greater than the damage from the event itself. The damage we do comes from our self-inflicted state of disbelief and pain. We are in a state of shock and awe that vibrates through every cell of our body. Depending on the circumstances, the power of anticipation does not guarantee our success in every venture because success is also correlated with our execution. However, even if we fail, the power of anticipation guarantees that we will not end up in such a fragile and depressed state of mind. The practice of anticipation will give us the benefit of conserving our morale and mental health in order to move beyond the carnage and fight another day.

# 3

## PURA VIDA

*And why should we feel anger at the world?*
*As if the world would notice!*
— Euripides

We live in a society that urges us to have more of everything. More likes and followers on social media, more money, more clothes, more cars, more, more, more. Because of this, it is hard for us to feel that we have enough of anything. We lose sight of what we have and focus on what we don't have. Even the things that we have, we feel that we don't have enough of them because we keep getting bombarded with the realization that other people have much more than we do.

This does not just apply to physical things, it also applies to the closest people in our lives. I have heard people complain about their parents, wishing they were just as open-minded and flexible like their friends' parents. This reduces our appreciation for our own parents, and we start viewing them as incomplete and something we were unfortunate to end up with. I have seen people do similar comparisons with their boyfriend or girlfriend when they met someone else's. A comparison is immediately made, their lover suddenly falls below the bar, and from that point on they start viewing them as inferior. If only they could be just as stylish, attractive, or fit as that other person. Instead of being happy to have them, they now have them because that is all they are able to have at this point.

How can we feel grateful for anything with such a way of looking at our lives? Social media makes it even harder for us to feel grateful. We spend hours every day scrolling through other people's lives, those whom we know and those whom we don't. We see all the things that we lack, the life we wish we had. We see the exotic places they are visiting while we are stuck at the office working. We see the super fit body they are showing off while we are struggling to find the discipline to workout. We see the events we have not been invited to, the huge number of followers we don't have, it goes on and on.

No wonder it's hard for most people to feel happy these days. And whenever they do feel happy, it doesn't last very long because we have deprived ourselves of the state of mind that is essential to our well-being: feeling grateful. Gratitude is not a synthetic feeling that you manufacture, and it is not something that you lie to yourself about. It comes from a deep conviction that you have so much to feel grateful for, regardless of how little you have. When you are truly grateful, you are rarely distracted by the many things you see on social media which you currently lack because your thinking is too focused on how what you have is more than enough.

According to the Happy Planet Index 2019 survey, Costa Rica is the happiest country in the world. You could argue that one of the biggest reasons Costa Ricans are the happiest people in the world is because they experience and practice gratitude more than any other people in the world. Costa Ricans practice gratefulness in every encounter they have with a friend or a stranger, with every conversation they have. Their secret is in "Pura Vida."

If you visit Costa Rica, you will notice that this phrase is uttered frequently—it's used to say hello or goodbye or even to convey that everything is alright. The direct translation of Pura Vida is pure life or simple life. However, to Costa Ricans it is much more than that. To them Pura Vida is a way of life, it is the attitude they credit for what has made them the happiest people in the world. Pura Vida means that, instead of dwelling on the negative things that are happening in their life, people need to dwell on the positive things instead. People who practice Pura Vida understand that no matter how bad you think your life is going, there are other people who have it much worse and would happily trade your life for theirs in a split second.

That means there are so many good things in all of our lives that we are not conscious of and we need to practice Pura Vida to realize how fortunate we are. Pura Vida is the same pathway that ultimately leads to happiness. Anticipating the negative is being conscious of how things could become worse. Pura Vida is being grateful that they have not. They complement each other, not contradict.

You might look at your life and wonder, what is it about my life that people might like so much that they would be willing to trade their life for mine? Well, we can start with the very first day you were born. What kind of life were you born into? Was it a place that lacks access to clean water, basic sanitation, and shelter? There are hundreds of millions of people who have lived their whole lives without these things that most of us take for granted. Were you born into a war torn place, where you or your loved ones could get shot on the street if you got caught in the crossfire?

Most people that have everyday luxuries such as heat and clean water, never think about how fortunate they are. They take such luxuries for granted. But imagine your life without these gifts—could you withstand it? We need to be grateful for those privileges in our lives every day because there are hundreds of millions of people who are forced to struggle and withstand how punishing life becomes when stripped of these basic necessities.

The point is not to make you feel guilty for being upset or unhappy despite the luxuries you enjoy. Instead, the point is to make you feel more happy by discovering the many gems in your life that you still have to smile upon despite everything else that might not be going well. The act of feeling grateful is a therapeutic exercise that calms your nervous system and releases happy hormones in your brain. To gain the benefits of this exercise we must do it regularly, and it is hard to do it regularly if we're waiting for big leaps in life to feel grateful for, because those don't happen on a daily basis. That is why we must feel grateful for the more basic things in our lives.

Not to mention that the day might come where those basic needs might be stripped from you. There are many countries worldwide that were doing very well and never expected to experience a war when overnight their citizens were turned into refugees, fleeing from death. Before the COVID-19 pandemic, people who lived in some of the most expensive addresses in the world in the heart of New York City and San Francisco never imagined that their location could ever be a disadvantage. When the enforced lockdowns went on for months, they suddenly found themselves feeling like they were living in a prison cell because of their small apartment that they were not allowed to leave. Even the most basic things that you take for granted, which you find it hard to feel grateful for today, could be taken away from you tomorrow, including your freedom and your health.

It might be hard to think of ourselves as privileged because we have always looked above our circumstances, toward people that are even more privileged than we are. Now we need to realize that even those people we look up to have other people above them that are more privileged than they are, and the cycle continues. Instead, we need to be conscious of those who are less privileged than us so that we can truly feel grateful for everything we have, much of which we don't even realize.

Practice scanning your life for everything that is good instead of focusing on what your life lacks. Remember the good health that you have, even if you have a certain illness or disease, remember the many more diseases that you have been spared from. Think of the education you have been granted, the opportunity to work and learn, the family and friends surrounding you. Ultimately, think of the privilege of being alive, of being able to feel and experience so many things. Dwell on the fact that your life still goes on, that you still have a chance to rectify whatever mistakes bother you, a chance to make more memories, to experience more things. Once we establish a mountain of things we're grateful for, anything negative happening in our life will feel like a pebble falling on a mountain. It will almost have no effect. But remember, gratefulness or Pura Vida is an ongoing attitude, it is something you have to practice every day for it to work.

When you feel grateful for what you have, you will feel a calm and happy energy running through your body, calming your senses, putting you in a relaxed state and eventually drawing a happy smile on your face. When you have practiced this energy for long enough, people can feel it in you and will enjoy being around you. You will attract more people into your orbit because of the positive and happy energy radiating from you. More positive people will enter your orbit, as will more opportunities.

Gratefulness will have a magic healing effect on your life as well as the lives of others who can feel your energy. An air of peace and joy descends on a person that is truly grateful despite whatever calamities might be going on in their life.

Feeling grateful is what has allowed me to survive the most difficult times in my life. I have lost all my money before. Gratefulness is what got me past suffering from my biggest losses. I realized that no matter what I lost, even if it was all my money, I still had so much more to smile about.

I see a lot of young entrepreneurs envious of other entrepreneurs that have managed to raise tens of millions of dollars from investors early in their career. When you are truly grateful, next time you hear a story like that you won't feel any envy, you won't feel that you are falling behind. Instead, you will find yourself automatically smiling on people's fortunes. Others will notice that in you because it is a rare sight. When you are grateful, your sense of fulfillment does not shrink as you scroll through social media and see all the things that others have which you don't. When you are grateful, you are a mountain that is not shaken by the storms, the thunder or the lighting.

Go on now, arm yourself with the sword and shield of gratefulness, practice it every day. Once you do, you will have picked up a superpower that few people are aware of.

# 4

# WHAT YOU SEE IS NOT WHAT'S IN FRONT OF YOU

*A good person dyes events with his own color.*
*And turns whatever happens to his own benefit.*
— Seneca

And there she was in the distance. . . I had never met her before but I felt like I knew her. I felt something more than that. Something I shouldn't have felt. We made eye contact but I didn't go up to her. I wanted to talk to her but she was surrounded by too many people, and I don't like being in a queue. Celebrities, wealthy businessmen, and famous athletes all lined up to congratulate the new world champion. She put on a tremendous display of talent and valor. Everyone was impressed by her dramatic performance.

She was the underdog before the game even started, and she lost the first few games to her ruthless opponent, the world's best, who was looking to finish her off in the last game of the night. I watched her from the front row of the VIP section, fighting her way back throughout the match, refusing to give in despite the injuries she suffered in the game. She started to win one game after the other in the most unlikely manner. I saw so much of myself in her. She played the game with so much vitality combined with such elegance, relentlessness, and emotion. A rare combination. I fell under her spell, as I felt I was looking at myself in the mirror. I'd never heard of her or followed her sport until that eventful night that changed everything. The last time I had followed this sport was five years earlier when I watched the world championship on site in New York.

The next day, I found myself thinking of her. Why is she still on my mind? I do not like it when something controls me like that. What was bothering me was the fact that I did not meet her in person. Yes, the large crowd swarming her was not how I like to meet someone of interest, but at the same time I completely missed my chance to meet her. We had so much in common; such coincidences do not come by often. I could have surely found a way to arrange an audience with her, as I always manage. Alas, what is done is done, I thought. I must forget about her, unless she magically pops into my life again. That will be my cue that there is something I should pursue.

Less than two hours later, while taking a walk, I see her walking toward me. I found it hard to believe my eyes. She walked into a store halfway between us and I walked in right after her without hesitation. I see her standing two meters in front of me. She is even more attractive off the court. What am I doing? I asked myself. I should just walk out. . .

Not in a million years. I approached her and started a conversation. We found a couple of chairs and chatted for an hour, then I walked her to the car that was waiting for her. She said she was supposed to travel an hour ago after picking up something from the store, but she stayed when she met me, she had noticed me yesterday at the world championship. She gave me her number and asked me to call her next week when we would both be in the same city.

I am still in disbelief about how the stars managed to line up on their own like this. Before I had left my house, I was planning on shaving my beard, but I decided not to last minute. Had I shaved my beard, I would have never met her. I would have arrived at the store ten minutes after she left.

The week went by slowly, we messaged throughout, and the day finally came for us to meet again. I booked us a lunch, though I didn't want it to seem like anything serious. I still wanted to get to know her first to reaffirm some of the ideas I had about her. She showed up dressed up like it was a date. She looked gorgeous in her dress and the first thing she said was how we both arrived at the restaurant at the exact same second. She sat next to me on the couch as we looked at one menu together. It was a total date. I didn't expect it to start out like that. I was planning to just feel her out, but it seemed she had already decided she was going on a date. It went on for five hours. Maybe longer if you count the extra time after she insisted on driving me home and the time we took to aimlessly cruise around the city while listening to music.

She asked when she would see me next, and I said it would have to be in the next few days because I was traveling for a month after. Her heart seemed to drop. She yelled, "You will not be here for the last tournament of the season?!" I said, "Unfortunately not. Unless," I added, "it would make a big difference if I was there." She said of course it would. I smiled and asked her, "How big of a difference?" She smiled back as she realized I was teasing her. We agreed that I would fly in for the tournament if she made it to the semifinal so I could be with her during the two most important games.

The next day she called me and said she was out with her family and she wanted me to come by to meet them. I obliged. We spent hours together past midnight, and then I said I had to go because I needed to get some sleep. They seemed to be disappointed. They wanted more time together. Her mother suggested that we should meet again before I traveled in two days. She asked me to choose the day and the time and that they would be there. "What about your daughter's rigorous training schedule?" I asked. She said, "We will cancel it if it conflicts. You are much more important." Apparently, she was very close to her mom, who managed her sports career and took care of everything for her.

I found it hard to believe how fast things were progressing. Here was a world champion who regularly met all kinds of important and influential people, yet somehow she decided to quickly and strongly pursue me, which made me feel like this was some kind of divine intervention. The probability of all of this happening was close to zero—with one hundred zeros on the other side of the decimal point. Yes, it's still a zero, but a much more dramatic one.

I was a really gifted athlete when I was in high school. My dad played on the national soccer team. It was in my genes. Any sport I picked up, I naturally excelled in it. So many coaches said I would be world champion one day. But in my senior year in high school, I decided I wanted more from life than the world cup. So, I gave up sports and pursued a career in entrepreneurship. As the years went by, I looked back often and wondered how my life would've been different had I pursued a career in professional sports. There were things for me to experience on the field, battling like warriors, that the business world could never give me. As I was spending time with her, I felt like I could vicariously live the professional sports life I missed out on through her. With all the life experience I had, all my knowledge of psychology and neuroscience, I could give her a bulletproof mindset that would make her unstoppable. With me behind her, she could transcend her sport, she could become the biggest female athlete in the world. That gave me an additional sense of purpose.

Just a few months before meeting her, I was reflecting on how my whole life was voluntarily filled with so much risk and danger. I enjoyed it on the edge, it made things exciting, I handled pressure very well and almost seemed to enjoy it. My friends even made up a word after me. "Sherifocist": someone who gains pleasure from high risk or dangerous situations. After a few decades of that, I was ready to turn the page, start a new chapter for a change. I wanted stability. A friend of mine told me that if I really want stability I should consider marriage. When you have your own family, you will think twice before you put them or yourself through anything risky or dangerous. That was the first time I'd ever heard a valid argument for marriage. I always felt the concept was not for me, and if I were to ever get married it wouldn't happen before I turned forty, or maybe even after. Now I was convinced that the right marriage would help me change my lifestyle from dangerous to stable. So, it wasn't far-fetched that when I met her shortly after changing my mind about marriage, I felt that destiny was telling me that it was all coming together and she might be the one.

As much as I would have liked to see her again, I thought canceling her training was not the right thing to do, so I called her and told her that it wouldn't work out for us to meet before I left but that we'd have plenty of time to make up for it when I got back. She said, "We are going to do everything when you are back anyway." When her mom got word, her mom insisted that she wanted to drive me to the airport since it was the only way for us to see each other before I left. "No way," I said. "My flight is at two in the morning!" In response, she said, "It's OK, I don't sleep early anyway." I must have refused her request on the phone at least six times, but she insisted.

Out of politeness, I obliged, but on only one condition, that she would not bring her daughter because I felt she needed to get a good night's sleep and rest from all her hardcore training. She agreed on the condition and asked me to send her my location.

On her way to pick me up, she called me to ask what kind of coffee I would like. I insisted that she not bother herself with bringing me any coffee. "OK," she responded. "I will bring you something better than coffee." She showed up with her daughter in the car. I think the last time anyone drove me to an airport other than a driver was my parents in college. This was so unreal. It cemented all the ideas I had formed in my head. She really is the one; she is much younger than me, so she can wait for me even four years for me to get comfortable with the concept of marriage; she has her own career which she will be busy with during that time; we have plenty of time to get to know each other. Her mother said that her husband was arriving tomorrow and she was considering going to the beach that day so someone else should pick him up from the airport. I was so flattered that she cared so much to drive me to the airport—a courtesy that wasn't even granted to her husband.

I couldn't believe how my world could completely change in just one week. My female friends were joking that they expected to be at my engagement party in a couple of months. I recall I had booked my return flight to coincide with her semifinal. I knew she would make it, but I didn't tell her that so she didn't take my return for granted; I wanted to give her an incentive to win. The night before the semifinal, I called her. "Welcome back!" she exclaimed. "I'm not back yet," I said. She couldn't believe it. She was saying, "What? You're kidding!" In disbelief, she must have said that five times. She said, "My semifinal is tomorrow!" "No problem," I said. "I'll find a flight and I'll come back later today." I looked at the time my flight was supposed to arrive and we agreed that we would meet at her hotel at eight o'clock the night

I got in. We joked around for the rest of the call and I told her I'd call when I landed.

I called her when I landed but she didn't pick up. I sent her a message telling her I had arrived and was heading to her hotel, which was an hour and a half from the airport by taxi. When I was close to her hotel, I sent her a message saying I was there. I knew a friend who lived in the area, so I decided to go to his place until she called back. She had told me she had a lot of media interviews and she was receiving an award that night and I assumed her phone wasn't with her. An hour later, I decided to call her again, but she didn't pick up. That was my last attempt to reach her. The next day, I watched her play the semifinal on TV. To this day, I never made another attempt to reach her and I never heard back from her or her mom.

### Analysis

As a reader you might be confused, possibly shocked. That was the reaction of my handful of friends who knew about this story. They just couldn't process the plot twist. They gave me a lot of credit for how I handled it. They said most guys would have responded with either vindictive messages or desperate ones asking for an explanation. Doing neither was the winning response. Doing this while being a sensitive man was not easy. Being sensitive in such a chaotic world requires some really tough skin, alligator skin, which I have had to develop over time. There is more to say about what happened in that period, but it would probably make her identity more recognizable, and I would not like to defame someone.

There are two parts to the analysis of this story. The first part is their unethical behavior, a part that we will ignore. The second part is the effect that it had on me, which we will discuss. So, going back to the thoughts in your head, what happened? How does this story make any sense? Let us rewind to find out.

Apparently, what I was seeing was not actually happening. I was interpreting the events differently, inaccurately. But why was I seeing something different from what was happening in front of me? Isn't seeing as simple as walking? Don't our eyes naturally see what is in front of us? Well, we've probably assumed that all our life but the answer is no.

Your eyes are biologically part of your brain—they are just protruding outside and are located on your face, but they are actually part of the brain. So, the eyes send a picture made up of small pixels to the occipital lobe, which is the part of the brain that controls vision; and then the brain decides what to make of that picture. Basically, the brain decides what you see. Funnily enough, it's not the object in front of you that gets the privilege of being portrayed how it actually is, it is your brain that decides. This decision is made based on many other parameters, like what is going on in your head, your past experiences, future plans, etc. This is why different people can encounter the same thing yet experience it very differently.

If we take my story as an example, my brain was highly influenced by the concept of destiny or divine intervention. The next day after the tournament, when I coincidentally ran into her, the fact that I was just thinking about her less than two hours before—and told myself that I must forget about her unless she magically walked into my life—had me convinced that meeting up with her was nothing short of fate. Later on, when I saw how her mom was throwing herself all over me as a total catch and suitor for her daughter, just minutes into meeting me, reinforced my divine intervention theory. As a very spiritual person, that made me biased.

Another factor that influenced my vision was the nostalgia I had for my sports career and how badly I wanted to relive it. Instead of living it myself, I could now vicariously live it through her, as her mentor, as her backbone, helping her push past her limits. Seeing how everything was falling in place at the same time, given how unlikely it was for such events to take place, my vision was also influenced by another element—the fact that I had only started considering marriage just a few months before. My brain seemed to explain everything so perfectly, and all the pieces of the puzzle fit in. What we learned at the end of the story was that while there was just one possible explanation in my head, there could have been a hundred others.

## Frameworks

It was clear at the end of the story that the one explanation my brain had settled on was the only one that was certainly not true. Thus, we must learn to be alert in real time. While we are perceiving things, consider that there could be other explanations regarding what we are experiencing unfold in front of us. Instead of sticking to the explanation that we want to believe, we must remain open.

There is something called "confirmation bias." It is when we find evidence that confirms what we want to believe. There might have been some red flags in the story I told you. But people will usually veer toward information that confirms the rosy scenario they are looking for without realizing it. If we equally considered the possible negative interpretations of the events unfolding as we do with the rosy interpretations, we would tread more carefully.

Had I learned to "think negatively" for instance (see chapter 2), I would have considered that her mother's actions might not be genuine. That the mother and the daughter might not be true to the code of ethics and sportsmanship that they claimed to live by. That she might just have been enjoying the moment as opposed to being serious.

So, the first step in the framework is to ask yourself, what do you see? The second step is to ask yourself, could the same events be seen differently? Could there be other explanations to what you are seeing? Write them all down. Are any of your explanations influenced by past experiences or future aspirations? Make note of that.

Next, you must look for red flags, any events or behavior that seem strange, that don't fit in with the big picture. You might have overlooked this initially out of your strong belief in the big picture, where we tend to throw out the little things that don't fit in. It is these little things that might be your cue, your savior from falling victim to your own biases or other people's selfishness or cruelty. Look into these little things more deeply. Give them greater importance. Do they make the case for another explanation other than the initial one that you were more attached to? Do these little things make the case for any of the alternative explanations that you wrote down?

**We see inwards instead of outwards**

One of the most powerful, life-changing realizations that most people go through life without being aware of is that you don't see what is in front of you; you see what is in your head. There is a significant difference between the actual events that unfold in front of you and what you think you saw. This mostly has to do with events that involve people, because we harbor all kinds of assumptions, expectations, and judgements when it comes to people, whether we are aware of this or not. All these harbored feelings influence how we interpret people's actions and the situations we find ourselves in.

This does not just apply to our direct interactions with people, it also applies to our perception of our whole life as well. That includes where we think we are heading, and what we just came out of—our perception of this can be very different from what is actually happening in our life. For example, someone that keeps getting fired from one job to another might start believing that the world is against him. The evidence to him is clear; every time he is given a chance, someone comes along and deprives him of it. Instead of being more self-aware and looking into his behavior that might have gotten him fired to see if there is a trend, most people find it easier to quickly form a hardened opinion that the world is against them. In reality, they might have been showing up consistently late to work, they might have been very difficult to work with, etc.

Seeing what is in our head instead of what is actually in front of us is like driving a car while wearing goggles that show us a completely different city than the one we are in. It can be catastrophic! We think we are supposed to take a right where, in reality, we are about to turn right into a building. The irony is that this is how most of us live life. There is a huge gap between the reality we live in and the one that exists in our heads. The more we doubt that this applies to us, the more likely that this gap exists.

The fact that people argue a lot, over small or big things, provides further evidence for this wide disconnect between reality and our perception. People constantly argue over whose fault something was or who was to blame because they all interpreted the events that unfolded in different ways. Everyone is living in their own reality and they see everything that happens around them and to them through their own unique lens. This lens is the product of their whole cumulative experience in life and because everyone experiences life differently, the lens from which they look out on the world and interpret events is different as well.

The unique lens you use to perceive your reality is influenced by several parameters. Your ego is one. It determines how sensitive you are to the things that happened around you and how entitled you feel regarding how they should have turned out. Your past experiences are another as they usually determine a trend in terms of how you expect certain events to unfold or how you explain the intentions behind certain actions. Wishful thinking also plays a role in shaping this lens, where you sometimes magnify any grain of sand to indicate that what you wish for is what is happening. Finally, your self-image and your vulnerabilities also play a significant role. Given the uniqueness of all these elements to each person, the sum of them add up to a completely distinctive lens which allows no two people to experience and perceive the same events happening around them in the same way.

Be mindful of that when you are interacting with people. When you give them a compliment, they might think that you are making fun of them. When you are totally confused about why they misunderstood such a harmless comment, it might be because of previous experiences they had. It all leads back to the unique lens through which we all view our own lives.

### If you want to change your life, change your perspective

When it comes to our own lives, we sometimes feel paralyzed by events that we can't control. Events that were forced on us, events that we never expected that burden us. Perhaps what bothers us most is our complete inability to change those events. This could be a government ordered lockdown to contain a pandemic which forces us to stay indoors, or the sudden departure from our life of someone we cared very much about. Reversing such events is an insurmountable task. But inside our own mind it seems like we are bound to remain miserable until such events are reversed.

Instead of trying to move mountains, one must realize that the happiness we seek lies not in changing the events around us, but rather in changing our lens. For it is this lens that caused us such unhappiness in the first place. Any time we experience pain or unhappiness is a time for self-reflection, it is a cue that there is something in our lens that must be fixed and we should direct our energy internally to find it. What is causing this pain? It is usually not the external events, so we must look inside. Is it some self-held belief which we need to let go of? Is it an unreasonable expectation? Is it some unjustified assumptions we made? Is it our ego screaming out? Unless it is physical pain from a car that has run us over, we will usually find the answer to the pain we are suffering on the inside.

You will find that your ability to shift your perspective and change how you are perceiving the events around you is a superpower that can eliminate the pain or distress you feel from almost any situation. Instead of waiting until you are experiencing pain to recalibrate your lens, aim to recalibrate your outlook on a regular basis. Every time you are experiencing a worthy incident in your life, something that feels significant, you must remind yourself of this. Ask yourself, what am I seeing?

Is what I am seeing really what is happening or is it just
my perception? What could be other alternatives for
what is actually happening? Is the person I'm talking to
really attracted to me or are they just being nice? Or are
they pretending to be attracted to me because they are
trying to get something out of me? Is this client really
going to close the deal or are they just showing interest
to keep the door open? Is what we think is unfolding in
front of us what is actually happening or is it just what
we want to happen?

Once we have considered other alternatives to a situation, we must now trace back to the reason we might
have mistaken reality. Was it wishful thinking, or a deep
desire to be loved that is unfulfilled? Was it our ego that
makes us think everyone is after us? It is important to
trace the source so we can fix it.

You might find yourself in very hurtful situations,
where the only thing you can change is your perspective
and the situation will immediately change afterwards.
Let's look at an example. You just discovered that your
longtime girlfriend you were about to marry has been
cheating on you for a very long time and you didn't know
about it. The first thing you think of is how embarrassing
it's going to be for your friends and social circle to find
out. It kills you that there is nothing you can do about
this, the damage has been already done, she has cheated
over and over again, choosing another man over you in

secret and making a fool out of you. This feels like a reality you are stuck with. There is no way you can get out of this situation. There is nothing she can do to reverse the damage—it has already been done.

Well, what if you actually had the power to change the situation? By changing your perspective. Instead of perceiving the event as a disaster, why don't you perceive it as an awakening. Here is someone you thought was loyal, that you trusted and had your best interest in mind. In reality, they were lying and cheating behind your back. It is a gift that you woke up to this real knowledge as opposed to continuing to live a lie for more years or even making a bigger mistake and marrying this person. You now view it as a relief that this moment of awakening has happened before you got tangled up more deeply with this person. Thank god she's your girlfriend, not your wife! If she were your wife, your perspective would be thank god she's just my wife and not the mother of my kids, thank god we don't have any children together that would have to suffer through this messy divorce for the rest of their lives.

As soon as you have changed your perspective from negative to positive, you have opened the door for the pain to start going away. All the dark clouds will start to vanish. You had the power to change the situation, without changing anything about the situation, by simply changing your perspective. What a superpower!

Once you are out of the dark zone of feelings and can feel well again, now you're in shape to start the analytical part. Start by reflecting on your behavior in the relationship that might have led to this infidelity or failure of the relationship. It doesn't always have to be that you were responsible for it, but it is always good to do a mental replay and watch yourself from the outside with your ego on the sidelines. Sometimes you can see things in your behavior that were not obvious to you in real time.

# 5

# DON'T FIND YOUR PASSION

*Great passions are maladies without hope.*
— Goethe

Find your passion. You've been told that so many times. You know what I have to tell you? Don't. Don't find your passion. Because it will probably kill you. Instead of finding something you are passionate about, find something that gives you meaning and purpose instead. There is a big difference between passion and purpose. On the surface they might look the same, but fundamentally it is the difference between life and death. Let us look at the dangers of passion. You have come across them many times but may have never made the connection.

You fall in love deeply with someone, and the passion is almost like a fire that you can feel inside you. This burning passion leads you to overlook many things, rush in when you shouldn't have, and it blinds you at the end. When the fire dies and all that is left is the ashes, you look back and ask yourself, how did I not see this coming? How could I have made such decisions that were so obviously stupid but seemed right at the time. The answer is that passion blinds you and that is why it is very dangerous. That is why you should never find your passion.

Another example is an athlete that is so passionate about her sport, who gets injured two weeks before a competition. The doctors tell her that she has to rest and skip out the competition. "I can never do that," she says to the doctors. They just don't understand, she thinks. This sport is her life, she has been training for this competition day and night for so long, she can never sit it out. The passion she has for the sport burns so brightly, deep inside her, what would be the point of living if she doesn't compete in this tournament? There is no question about it, she is definitely going to compete and nothing can change her mind. That is the obvious decision to her anyway. She joins the competition and makes her injury much worse. It now needs months of healing instead of a few weeks. It also turns the injury into a long-term weakness that pops up every year when she stresses that muscle too much.

Now let us take a closer look at the difference between passion and purpose and the very different effects they have on our lives. We saw what passion leads to; as warm as the fire of passion might feel, it always leads to getting burned. We saw what happened to the athlete. Now imagine if she was driven by purpose not passion. She would know that her purpose is to be the most skilled player in her game, to improve the sport itself, to take it to a higher level, and to inspire new people to play the game and enjoy the sport. She would know that she needs a lot of time to do that, and so it is critical that she maximize the number of years she can play the game, and her ability to minimize injuries is a crucial part to achieve this longevity. When that injury came, her priority would have been to recover from that injury as opposed to participating in the tournament. She could always participate in the tournament next year, she would think, but any permanent damage that she inflicts on her body would be irreversible.

That is the difference between passion and purpose. Both of them motivate you, give you meaning, allow you to get out of bed early with a smile on your face ready to dive deep into the thing you love most. But one of them has very dangerous side effects that most often lead to disasters. Leave passion for the inexperienced. Find your purpose instead. Now let's talk about how you can find your purpose before you get destroyed by your passion.

# 6

## WHAT OF YOUR PURPOSE?

*Many people die at twenty-five and*
*aren't buried until they are seventy-five.*
— Benjamin Franklin

What are most people living for today? What are they trying to achieve? What do they dream about? Fame? Getting Rich? These are examples of a false purpose. These are things that never provide fulfillment or contentment. It is also almost impossible to attain them when you are trying to attain them directly. You are much more likely to find them when you are trying to achieve something more profound that results in fame or wealth as a byproduct as opposed to trying to be famous as the direct goal. For instance, wanting to be the most skilled pianist in your country is much more likely to result in you actually being a great piano player and being famous for it relative to wanting to be a famous piano player.

So what should we live for instead if not for the materialistic things that we crave or need? We have learned what a false purpose is, but what is a real purpose then? Real purpose has several qualities. First, it is something that comes from within you as opposed to having been imposed on you by someone else or by society. Second, real purpose aligns with something that you are naturally good at. Something that you feel very little to no resistance when you try to do it. Third, real purpose gives you meaning and makes you feel fulfilled every time you do it. Living with purpose does not have to be grand. Examples of a life filled with purpose could be raising your children well or relieving people's suffering. Other examples could be reducing poverty and increasing access to basic education.

When you are living with purpose you transform yourself from a person on a job into an unstoppable force. When your work aligns with your real purpose you are much more likely to withstand any dark clouds. You will find yourself easily able to work longer hours if needed and to produce a greater quality of work. Your managers will notice your extra level of dedication and commitment that stands out among your colleagues, and thus it will be easier for you to attain a promotion and be recognized by your managers. Once you align your job with your real purpose it is like transforming from a mercenary army that is only fighting because it is getting paid to a national army that is fighting to protect the freedom and dignity of a country. Which army do you think will win if both were equally equipped? History has shown that a national army fighting for a cause could defeat a mercenary army even if it was outnumbered and out equipped by the mercenary army! You will benefit from this multiplier effect if you pursue a career that is fueled by a real purpose.

How do you find this performance enhancer? How do we find our real purpose? There are several ways. It is like putting a puzzle together; there is no immediate way to find out. Here are several pieces of the puzzle. Notice the tasks, activities, or fields that you are naturally very good at, where you don't have to make much effort to get it right, you are a natural. This could be sports, cooking, getting along with people, helping people with their problems. It could also be mathematics, negotiation, sales, etc. List all the things that feel like you were born to do based on how good you are at it. Another dimension to look at is how much you enjoy doing certain tasks or activities. You could spend hours doing them, you feel no resistance whatsoever to sink yourself into them, you feel at home. A third dimension is the things you've been intrigued by and inclined to pursue since a very young age, before there was much influence from society on what you should do with your time. A fourth dimension is your inclination to pursue certain activities, projects, or careers at a more recent stage in your life after you had time to analyze and think them through.

Now you should list all the things you came up with under each pillar and see what overlaps. It is like a crossword puzzle—you will find a trend. For instance, someone might have discovered that they love helping people. They could spend hours on the phone or in person listening to their problems and giving them advice. They also realized that they like learning new things and are very good at writing. Such a person could research and write self-help programs as a real purpose. This doesn't have to be their only real purpose, but it is one that they would do well at and would allow them to live a meaningful life that they would enjoy, along with an increased chance of success.

The same person could do many other things that include working at a nonprofit that helps marginalized communities. They could be creating curriculums and programs for the nonprofit to implement. You can see the many possibilities one person has to live a life full of purpose. It is important that you look beyond the titles and the branding. Instead of looking for accounting, marketing, or sales jobs, think about real purpose in the way we broke it down in the previous example. See what kind of job could land you as opposed to the other way around. What do your options look like? Don't be alarmed if your purpose does not hit you instantly. It can take years to find your purpose or much less.

You only live twice. Once when you were born, and once when you start living…

# 7

## NEVER CHASE YOUR DREAMS

*It ain't what you don't know that gets you into trouble.*
*It's what you know for sure but just ain't so.*
— Mark Twain

They tell you to chase your dreams. You feel good about that because it makes you think of yourself as a go-getter, as unstoppable. Do you know where you are going to end up after chasing your dreams? Possibly just another burned-out prodigy who had so much talent. You felt that you almost touched the stars but you came a few inches too short. If you try chasing your dreams, you will probably spend your whole life chasing them and you will never reach them. Don't chase your dreams. As a matter of fact, don't chase anything. Let's explore why.

We live in an extremely fast-paced world—one that is changing faster than it ever has. When you set your eyes on a goal, perhaps at the time you took your first aim, it was the right goal for you. A few months into your pursuit of this goal, the world had changed, and you probably changed as well. That goal might not be the best thing for you anymore. It also might not have been the best thing for you to start with, but you didn't know that. At the same time, that goal seems to be slippery. It's not falling into your hands. You keep missing it. While these might be signals that you should not pursue this goal any further, you have been raised in a society that glorifies slogans like "never give up," and "follow your dreams." In a way, our society glorifies suffering, most of which is unnecessary. So, you become fixated on chasing the goal, regardless of the consequences, because you don't want to feel like a quitter.

The problem of the chase is that it becomes emotional. It is not your intellect that is in control and making the decisions anymore, it is your emotions. You have to recognize that, contrary to what you would like to think, you don't know yourself very well. Actually, you know very little about yourself. As we age, we get to know ourselves better, but our understanding of ourselves is always a fraction of what actually exists. So, when you set out to pursue that goal, or that person, or that thing, you did so with the understanding that it's what was best for you. But because you actually don't know yourself well enough, your goal might not actually be good for you at all, although on the surface or from far away it might seem hard to think otherwise. Another reason why you shouldn't be chasing, is you don't have a good understanding of the goal or the person you are pursuing. You think you do, but you actually don't. Then there are the obstacles, the sacrifices, and the processes you are going to have to go through in order to reach it.

So instead of chasing your dreams, you should proceed toward them with force and caution, hand in hand. You need to keep your eyes wide open and maintain an alert attitude to the signals you are getting back once you start pursuing that goal. These will tell you whether this is the right thing for you or not. I am not telling you to be a bum and not pursue any goals. I am also not telling you to be a habitual quitter where you start and quit many things. It is one thing to abort something you are pursuing because you are too lazy to put in the work, and it is another thing to stop pursuing something because you realize it will actually harm you. That is not quitting, that is coming to your senses.

Let's take an example of a guy who meets a girl that he likes and decides to pursue her. After he got her number and started messaging her, she doesn't respond to his messages promptly or with much affection. He takes it as a challenge and thinks, "I will make her interested, she just doesn't realize what I am like yet." So, he spends days, weeks, even months trying. It's no fun, perhaps even miserable, all so that he can attain someone that he doesn't even know what she's truly like or whether she's actually good for him in the first place.

That has probably happened to you and many people you know while pursuing relationships or things. In this example, it's how you are wired that's automatically reacting; you have been programmed to respond this way. When she is not responding to you it triggers your ego to chase her more. Now the reason you are chasing her is not because she is good for you or because you actually want her, the chase is now being stimulated by neurotransmitters in your brain circuit firing in all sorts of wrong directions.

Instead, the right approach should have been to abort once you realized there was no mutual interest or unequal interest. If we had our head above our shoulders, we would have realized that. But because we're programmed to chase, we waste too much additional time on the wrong thing that we might never realize it's not the right thing for us until we get it.

Here's what to do instead. This applies whether you don't know what you should do, what you should go after, or whether you have a really good idea of what you should pursue. In both cases, if you are confident about it, go for it initially. If you have no idea what to pursue, choose something, anything, to start with.

Now look for the signals that are coming back. Are you good at it? Is it working? Are you achieving tangible progress? These signals are a crucial part of the analysis and the decision-making that should go into deciding whether or not you should continue pursuing this. Your initial decision to pursue this person or endeavor is not a lifetime sentence of chasing after it no matter what. It was a decision to pursue this, given the current information you have, and once additional information is available it will go into reassessing whether this is still the best course of action.

If you are not making progress, you should ask yourself why. Is it because you were slacking off? Because you didn't surround yourself with the right people? If so, then this is what you should fix instead of jumping ship. Be careful of finding too many justifications and excuses as to why it was not working in order to give it a sixth and seventh chance instead of aborting and moving to something or someone else.

Remember, pursuing something has a very high opportunity cost because it prevents you from pursuing something else. When you are stuck on pursuing something that is not the right thing for you, you are preventing the right thing from finding you because you are too busy with something else. So, sometimes it is better to do nothing than to do anything.

Our choice of goals can be our downfall or our triumph. Sometimes before we have even lifted a finger we have destined ourselves to doom. We can become our worst enemy when we want something so badly. It is like the tires of our car getting caught off-road in the desert sands. The more we try to spin our tires in the sand, the deeper they get stuck.

When we find that our deepest passions and desires are causing us nothing but trouble and pain, the best thing to do is to reexamine those desires. We can use this reexamination to explore a completely new direction and aim for something more suitable to our current life and our respective needs. The more attached you are to something that is causing you pain, the more suspicious you should be of it. It takes humility to realize and accept that what you originally wanted was either not good for you or was not possible to have in the way you imagined.

# 8

# EMOTIONAL PAIN

*Choose not to be harmed and you won't feel harmed,*
*don't feel harmed and you haven't been.*
— Marcus Aurelius

How many times have you heard somebody say, "You made me angry!" or "You hurt me!" You've probably said it many times yourself. What is the problem with this statement? The problem is that it is scientifically invalid. Yes, people may do things that are inappropriate or uncalled for, but for those things to make you feel angry or hurt you, they require your permission.

Nobody can hurt you without your permission. Between the inappropriate action that has been taken by someone and the moment that you felt hurt or angry, there was a window of time in which several actions were taken by your subconscious mind at lightning speeds that made you complicit in feeling hurt. In that infinitesimal time between another's action and your emotional reaction, your brain made assumptions and decisions about the intentions of the person, and you made a subconscious verdict to feel angry or hurt.

So, in reality, nobody can make you angry or hurt, only you can do that to yourself. In the same window of time is your opportunity to pause, choose not to react, and choose not to be hurt. Nobody should be given the privileged access of pushing your buttons and commanding your reactions. People can be rude to you but you don't have to feel insulted or hurt about it. People can be late but you don't have to feel frustrated about it. This realization does not eliminate or reduce the wrong that they have done; that has already happened, and you can't take it away. What you can take away, however, and what has not happened yet, is a negative reaction that will serve no purpose other than making you feel bad and flooding your brain with negative emotions that might put your mood off for hours, days, or even weeks.

It takes a lot of training, but learning to manage your emotions and reactions will change your life. Do you realize how powerful you have just become? Previously your mood was greatly determined by so many factors outside your control. It was at the mercy of how pleasant people were around you. Your mood was controlled by whether they kept their promises and lived up to your expectations. If they did you were happy; if they didn't you were angry or even worse. So many people to interact with every day, so many things can go wrong—no wonder our moods are as fragile as glass.

That is a thing of the past now. With you taking back control of how you feel, your mood is only determined by one person. That person is you. Realize that you can't change people, just like it would be very hard for people to change you. You have to treat everyone like they have a unique set of traits, habits, and beliefs that have been forged over a long period of time. That's what makes them who they are. You can't change what is part of their fundamental fabric and you should not attempt to. Unless, of course, you would like to inflict some severe disappointment and mental suffering on yourself.

When you release your expectations of people to conform and behave in a certain way, you immediately free yourself of the disappointment that arrives when they don't (see chapter 1). You also need to decouple your self-image from how people treat you. If someone treats you in a way that you deem as disrespectful, it does not make you a person that is not able to command other people's respect. Their treatment says volumes about them, but it does not say anything about you. Once you learn to decouple your self-image from the actions of other people, it will be easier for you to take a pause before reacting because it is usually when your self-image gets hurt that sends a flare up your spine and triggers a strong reaction.

Let's look at a few stories that demonstrate this. Darren has an online meeting with his boss Kenny scheduled for two o'clock. It is 2:08 p.m. and Kenny has been waiting for Darren for eight minutes now. Kenny looks but does not find any emails or messages from Darren telling him that he is going to be late. These seconds start to feel like minutes for Kenny as he takes Darren's lateness and absence of communication as a sign of disrespect. "I am his boss after all," he says to himself. "How come I am the one that is sitting here waiting for him?" By the time Darren finally shows up and the meeting starts, Kenny is already too furious. While he has not expressed his fury out loud, it has already impacted the direction and dynamic of the meeting. All because Kenny linked Darren's lateness to his own self-image, by interpreting Darren's act of being late as a weapon aimed at Kenny, signifying his lack of respect for him.

Now let us visit this story with the healthy perspective of how it was supposed to go down. Darren did not necessarily mean to disrespect Kenny. His lateness could have been due to a million reasons. That goes for his inability to communicate that he was going to be late as well. He could have had problems with his internet, ran out of battery, so many things. Instead, Kenny should have just spared himself the unnecessary frustration he inflicted on himself as he waited for Darren to show up. What he could have done is simply message Darren telling him that he was waiting for him and proceeded to occupy himself with something productive until Darren showed up. Once Darren made an appearance, Kenny could have objectively explained to him that he likes punctuality and in the future, if Darren expects to run late, he should just message Kenny in advance to inform him of this. All without any negative feelings. In the first case, Kenny's mood suffered, the meeting dynamic suffered, and finally Darren probably suffered at the end. In the second case, nothing was lost.

With so many instant forms of communication like phones, messaging, and email, we now expect people to answer us instantly. When they take too long to answer, hours or even days, we get frustrated, upset, sometimes even hurt. Because we link the behavior of that person to our self-image and set our expectations for how we believe they are going to act. So we get anxious. Anxiety is another reaction that we choose. We start imagining scenarios to explain their behavior. Instead, we should abandon these unhealthy habits. If we need an urgent response for this specific instant, we can message or call the person again to communicate that need. But trying to change people's communication habits or linking their nature to our self-image is a recipe for an unhappy life.

# PART II

## CONTRARY TO COMMON BELIEF

# 9

# ATTACHMENT

*You become what you give your attention to.*
— Epictetus

What is attachment? It is the feeling that you can't live without something. When something has become so intertwined with your existence that you can't imagine your life without it, or at least you don't want to imagine your life without it. You don't ever want to part ways with it, whatever happens. That is attachment, and it is extremely unhealthy.

To discover why it's unhealthy or even borderline toxic, let us consider what happens when something you are attached to suddenly disappears from your life. You will be devastated. You will feel immobilized, you won't be productive, and you might not be able to work or focus or think about anything else. You certainly won't be yourself anymore, and the cost of that is too high and your responsibilities too many to risk this happening. That is why you need to scan your life for unhealthy attachments and eliminate them because they are like a gigantic time bomb waiting to detonate and tear your life apart.

There are several types of attachment. The first is attachment to people. You might be attached to someone you are romantically in love with. They give you butterflies, you are so deeply and madly in love with them. You can't imagine what life would be without them; it would be complete suffering. While romance is a lovely feeling, and it's great that you found someone who makes you feel like that, you are probably on your way to a disaster because statistically most romantic relationships fail. And what will happen when a relationship fails that you have been severely attached to? Depression and all its cousins suddenly arrive, and they might stay for months, sometimes even years.

Attachment to people can happen beyond romantic partners. You could be attached to your children, your parents, or your best friend. What happens when one of those starts to unconsciously take advantage of you to the point where they are decimating your mental health? If you are attached to them you will be stuck in a toxic loop of trying to explain to them how they are affecting you negatively, but they just don't get it and you continue to suffer.

When I use the term "attachment" I don't mean caring deeply for someone or something. In no way am I encouraging you to be cold, or heartless, or to have no feelings whatsoever. On the contrary, being able to feel and express emotion is one of the most beautiful things that we can experience as humans. It is one thing to have all kinds of positive emotions for people and things in your life, and it is another thing to reach a point where you can't function without those things in your life. The latter is obviously an unhealthy condition that needs to be rectified before it gets worse.

Beyond people, you could be overly attached to a job. For many people, their work has taken the center of their life. It is what gives them meaning, and they can't imagine their life without it. They pour themselves into their work, putting in long hours, working weekends, canceling any other plans if their work demands it. That is an example of an unhealthy attachment because it comes at the cost of other things in your life that are just as important. This attachment prevents the nourishment from other areas in your life needed in order for you to grow as a person. When you have an unhealthy attachment to your work, your social life will suffer, your family will suffer, and your health will suffer, and all that suffering happens while you still have your work.

Now imagine what happens when your work is taken away from you. You were fired, the company went bankrupt, you suffered an accident that prevented you from being able to conduct your work. A million things can happen that could take your work from you. What happens to you then? You will probably feel worthless because it was your work that filled up most of your life and now you feel a void. You start asking yourself what you are without your work. You realize how much you neglected all the other important areas of your life.

Attachment is very dangerous, but usually people only realize that after some serious damage has been done to them by what they were attached to. You need to identify those unhealthy attachments early and eliminate them before they eliminate you.

Attachment can come in many other forms that are just as dangerous. You could be attached to your pets, to a cause, or to an image of yourself. In the case of an image, let us say that you are attached to seeing yourself as someone who is always respected and revered in your community—people always view you as a role model. If an event were to happen that casts you in a different light, you might not be able to bear it because you were attached to a certain image of yourself. These are attachments that you must let go of as well.

Attachments to causes can also wreak havoc in your life. Growing up, I used to be fanatic about my Egyptian identity. I was the biggest patriot that you would ever meet. After all, with all the mysticism that surrounds

Egyptian history and the rich culture and civilization that has been built over thousands of years, it is hard not to fall under that spell. As a result of this unhealthy attachment to my Egyptian identity, when I traveled to the US for college and spent four years there, I did not attempt any paperwork to pursue a US green card or citizenship. I was so proud of my Egyptian identity that I was not willing to accept an additional citizenship on top of it. I used to tell myself as a college student that when I graduated and became famous I didn't want to be known as Sherife AbdelMessih, the Egyptian-American entrepreneur; I wanted to be the Egyptian entrepreneur, giving as much glory to Egypt as I could.

I graduated college on June fifth and was on a flight back to Egypt on June seventh, only because there was no flight on June sixth. Instead of taking advantage of the many opportunities I had to gain experience and work in the US or other more developed countries, I went back to Egypt immediately. That is where my sense of attachment brought me: my country needs me.

Years after graduation, I repeated the same mistake. The company I started grew and established subsidiaries on multiple continents. My meetings with presidents and ministers of powerful countries became more regular, and they were fascinated by the work I was doing in their countries. It would have been so easy to gain dual citizenship. But when the extension of such an honor was ever brought up by senior government officials, I would take it as an insult. I already had a country I belonged to; why would I need a second?

It took me decades to realize how much this unhealthy attachment hurt me. Having spent most of my career traveling more than nine months out of the year, it was such a hassle to apply for so many visas, as most countries require Egyptian citizens to apply for a visa. For practical reasons, a second passport that allowed me to visit more countries visa free and not having to leave my passport at a consulate for weeks in advance would have been essential. But I was happy to bear this burden for the pride of my Egyptian identity. Had I known about the mental health cost that came with this, I would have gotten a second passport since I was in college! Nobody taught me about unhealthy attachment back then.

We have seen examples of what attachment should not be like, but what should it be like instead?

## Once it burns don't hold on

For our own protection, our nervous system has been wired to automatically instruct our hands to let go of an object once it detects that the temperature is so high it is going to burn us. Can you imagine instead if, in the same scenario, our nervous system were to send a message to our brain saying, "The object you are carrying is too hot, you should let go of it"? By the time we think about it and make up our mind to finally let go of the object, our hands would already be burned.

Taking a cue from our biological design, whenever you feel that something is causing you pain, that's a sign that you have unconsciously attached to something. That is an attachment that you need to let go of, just like the hot pan. Instead, what most people do because they are not familiar with this attachment framework is continue holding the hot pan while talking to it as it is burning them. "Lower your temperature, you are hurting me, stop now I am in pain, can't you see what you are doing?!" That's what we do. How effective is that? Instead, drop the hot pan, then talk to it if you want.

Detaching from something isn't the same thing as abandoning it. Detaching is simply staying at a healthy distance so that you can continue to interact without hurting yourself. That distance can increase or decrease with time based on the results; it is not set in stone.

You need to mentally understand that the basic foundation of love is caring for each other, and you cannot regularly cause someone pain whom you care for. If you are frequently being wronged by someone you care for then the relationship needs a software update, and you need to step back to reassess. The second benefit to stepping back is that they will realize they can't take you for granted, that they must have done something wrong, and this will force them to reassess their actions as well, although it might take them time. This goes for all people in your life—family, friends, coworkers, romantic partners, etc.

You should focus on your side of the equation and not theirs. Love people, care for them, but don't be attached to them, for where there is attachment, suffering lies just around the corner.

## Scanning for attachments

It is time to think about the attachments that exist in your life. Who are the people you are attached to, whom you can't live without? List them all. The ones who, if gone, you wouldn't be able to function. It is one thing to say that you enjoy having someone in your life and it is another to say you wouldn't be able to function without someone in your life. The latter is a problem as it will immobilize you, and you need to identify and work on all such cases before it happens at a time when you are not prepared to deal with it.

In most cases, the reason you have attached to the people on your list is because they provide you with something that you lack. It does not have to be something materialistic, it could be emotional security or purpose.

You need to think about the reason why you attached to each of these people. The reason can't be something general like he's my father. There are millions of people that are not attached to their father, so that is not the reason. Dig deep into your mind. What is it that your father has been providing you with that has resulted into this deep attachment that you have with him? Go on, continue listing the things that come to your mind. You might not be able to do it all in one day as it will take time for you to be able to access everything that has been locked up in your subconscious. Do the same with everyone on your attachment list.

The result of this exercise is realizing the attachments that you need to rid yourself of. By finding the reasons that resulted in the attachment, you are also finding your homework for the things that you need to develop in yourself. For example, if you were attached to someone because they loved you so much, you need to learn to love yourself because it is something that you were lacking.

Love people deeply, just don't attach to them. There is a time where they will disappear from your life, either because your relationship with them has broken or because they simply died like everyone will. In either case, if you were attached to them, you will be devastated.

Do the same exercise of scanning for attachment in other areas in your life besides your relationships. Scan for attachments to causes, hobbies, work, self-image, pets, ideals, etc. This is not a one-time exercise. Get in the habit of monitoring such attachments and scanning your life on a regular basis every few months for new attachments that might have appeared.

# 10

## THE PRESENT TENSE

*The present is all we have to live in or to lose.*
— Leo Tolstoy

You would think it is obvious when we say live in the present, but you would be surprised by how few people actually do. Most people either live in the future, or even worse, live in the past. Every moment that is not lived in the present is a moment wasted, a time in your life that you will never get back. The past is behind you; you cannot get it back. The future will come; you can't have it now. The only thing you can have now is the present and if you lose it, you gain nothing.

So, what does it mean to live in the present? It is to be completely available, mentally and emotionally, to experience the present moment. If you are at lunch with friends, all your energy is spent appreciating the food you are eating and all your focus is engaged in the conversation at hand, instead of having half your attention stressed about your next appointment and the other half worried about how your last meeting went. Such behavior will not impact either activity. Instead, your stress and worry will negatively impact the present and you will miss the chance to fully experience what is in front of you, which will only exist in front of you for a limited time.

Ultimately, you have to understand that anything you can achieve in life can only happen in the present. So, if your senses are not located in the present to start with, then you have much less of a chance of achieving, fixing, or improving anything. The present is the only opportunity for real pleasure. Spending hours on fantasies about what tomorrow will bring or reliving old memories is like taking drugs. It might release dopamine and other happy hormones in your brain, but drugs do the exact same thing. The happiness you feel from both is not real and you will soon lose the pleasant effect it has on you. The only way to feel genuine and healthy happiness is by engaging in activities in the present.

Why do people live in the past? The specific reason changes from person to person, but they can be ultimately divided into two types of people. The first type is someone who lives in the past because of certain glory or power that they used to have which they don't have anymore. The only way they can relive that power is by reliving their past. The second type of person is someone who was severely hurt by an event in the past. They were so traumatized and have not fully recovered yet. They continue to relive these traumatic events as if they are still happening.

Both groups of people must understand that the past is behind them. There is nothing you can do about the past; it is gone. If there is anything you can actually do about it, it lies in present action, not lingering over past events and replaying them in your head. If you are suffering from events that happened in the past, ending your suffering lies in taking present action, such as getting professional help, reading self-help books, and engaging in anti-depression activities like sports and exercise.

If you are living in the past because your life used to be so much better, And if thinking about what it used to be like gives you a high as opposed to living in the sad reality of your present, that is not a solution. The only way to truly regain those glories is by rebuilding them in the present as opposed to reimagining them in your mind. The danger of living in the past in this case is that your mind will get so lazy because it has gotten used to gaining pleasure from replaying past events and realities which don't require it to do any work. On the other hand, getting off your couch and actually doing the work to rebuild those past glories requires a lot of effort. So, your brain will get you stuck in past glories and your situation will only get worse. Unless you stop feeding yourself cheap drugs and fantasies, the only way your brain can taste those happy hormones regularly will be from actual work and the results that come with it. Only then will you be forced to rebuild.

Those who live in the future do so to escape a mundane present as they look forward to a more exciting future. This could be someone who is about to start a new job and resign from an old one. In their last two months, perhaps all they can do is to think about how amazing the new job is going to be and they can hardly get themselves to do any work at the current job. To their surprise, once they start the new job, they might find themselves engaging in similar behavior, where now they are looking forward to something else and not engaging with their new job at all.

That is the danger of living in the future. You condition your brain to manufacture fantasies that you can feel and experience simply by sitting in your chair. You can experience anything you want through such fantasies—your boss recognizing your special abilities in front of all your coworkers, winning the best employee of the year at the company, etc. To experience these same things in real life requires a humongous amount of work. But you have trained your brain to say, why should I bother with all that work when I can just experience the same pleasure in my head? The end result is becoming a couch potato.

The longer you do this, the harder it is to stop. It is a form of an addiction.

The solution? To live exclusively in the present and nowhere else. The only answer to your problems or your dreams lies in the present. Let tomorrow worry about itself, deal with it when it becomes today, for now it is still tomorrow. Let the past rest where it belongs—in the past. Today is a day that can have a different outcome. It is up to you.

*We protect our money, and our property*
*but we squander our time.*
— Seneca

# 11

## NEGATIVE FANTASIES

*We suffer more in imagination than in reality.*
— Seneca

S tress and anxiety are the biggest pandemic humanity has ever experienced. It has infected people across all age groups, economic classes, and education levels. It does not matter what you do or how far you progress in life, two things always seem to be there: stress and anxiety. In the US for example, the world's biggest economy and arguably the biggest meritocracy, where the American Dream has always been alive and everyone believed they could be anything they want, stress and anxiety is on every corner. According to a 2021 study by the Kaiser Family Foundation, four out of ten US adults suffer from anxiety or a depressive disorder. If it is so bad in the US, imagine what it is like in the rest of the world, where it is harder to change your economic status for the better, and security and the rule of law is not as reliable.

Why is it that we experience such chronic stress and anxiety? Over the last few years the amount of stress and anxiety-inducing stimulants around us have grown at an exponential pace. However, our ability to deal and manage those stimulants in a healthy way has not grown, or worse has gotten weaker. We experience stress when there is something in our environment that is pressuring us, such as a deadline or an important meeting.

Anxiety, on the other hand, is the negative feeling that still remains after the pressure has been relieved. For example, still feeling anxious about the important meeting even though the meeting is finished. That feeling you have after the meeting is anxiety, not stress. Although both are equally harmful, anxiety might be easier to get rid of because some people work in environments that are naturally stressful, such as the quick-paced stock market or a busy restaurant kitchen. In such cases where the pressure is constant due to the nature of the job, we can only learn to let this pressure force us to focus on our job instead of being stressed about it.

A fantasy is a situation you imagine in your head that you wish was real. It is a situation that makes you feel good to imagine. Whether it is a place you wish you could go to or a person you wish you could be with, fantasies are assumed to be positive. However, there are also negative fantasies. You have them almost every day, you just know them under a different word—anxiety. You imagine negative situations that have not unfolded yet. Your mind plays every possible scenario of how things could go wrong and you get tortured by them. That is a negative fantasy. It is best to live in the present and not have any fantasies, but if you are going to have one, you might as well have a positive fantasy!

In order to rid ourselves from stress and anxiety, we first must realize and admit that this is a problem in our life. Some people don't even realize they experience stress and anxiety. I was such a person. I recall when I was in college in Boston, I noticed that every day I woke up there was a lot of hair on the pillow. The next time I went to get a haircut, I told my barber about this and asked him what was wrong with my hair. He responded with an answer that I thought was completely irrelevant and that I had just wasted my time asking him this question. He said that I was probably stressed and that it was natural for people to be stressed at a college like MIT. After all, we have a saying, "Studying at MIT is like drinking out of a firehose." I was expecting an answer that had to do with the nature of my hair or the nature of his work, a hairdresser after all. Simply blaming my hair loss on something like stress seemed to me like he knew nothing about hair and gave some generic answer instead of admitting that he doesn't know. All of that was because my subconscious mind was not willing to admit that I could actually be stressed! That I was being challenged to keep up with all the demands that come from being a very active student at MIT!

Stress continued to be a problem for me in my first few years of work after graduation, mainly because I continued to demand so much of myself and was always living in a self-imposed high-paced and high-pressure environment. But, more importantly, I still lacked the realization that I was experiencing a lot of stress. I always saw myself as someone with cool nerves and composure. I didn't realize my stress until I experienced a severe back spasm in the middle of a phone conversation. My whole back muscles suddenly jolted with the feeling of electricity. I fell to the ground and dropped the phone. I lay on my back for an hour because I couldn't move without pain. As I started wondering what could have led to this, I slowly became conscious of all the things that were happening in my life, and how stress builds up whether you realize it or not—it does not wait for your permission to enter and it will stay unless you make changes in your lifestyle.

The next step to eliminate stress and anxiety after we recognize that it exists is realizing the damage that it incurs on our lives. We waste hours feeling stressed and anxious, and in these hours we're not able to do much productive work or enjoy our time. They are hours lost that we can't get back. Losing such valuable time is not the only incurred damage—our health suffers greatly as well. In addition to the short-term damage to our health, which we can feel in our mood and the lack of quality in our sleep, there are many health studies that have linked accelerated aging and the growth of cancer to chronic stress and anxiety. At the end of the day, stress and anxiety leave us drained of energy and reduce our ability to respond well to the situations we are anxious about.

The third step to get over anxiety is to catch yourself in the moment when you are starting to feel anxious. Tell yourself, here I go again. And stop yourself from that negative train of thought. Remind yourself that, regardless of how bad the situation is, you only make it worse by being anxious about it. It is like pouring fuel on fire. You reduce your capacity to fight back and waste hours of your day where you are not able to think clearly. When something is causing you to have recurrent negative fantasies, ask yourself, can I do something about it? If the answer is yes, then why stress about it? Do something about it instead. If the answer is no, again why stress about it, you can't do anything about it, so let it go.

If stress is a result of a lot of pressure in your work or personal environment, then consider how sustainable it is to live under that level of pressure and make changes accordingly. If it is a short-term period, it can be manageable, but make sure to avoid the trap of saying something is only temporary, while in reality it has slowly turned into the norm. Check back in a few weeks or in a month on those "temporary" stressors; if they are still there, you must take action to eliminate them. You can eliminate them by asking the people involved to change their attitude which leads to stressing you out, or by eliminating such people or activities altogether.

This is another muscle that you learn to grow. Your goal should be to turn yourself into a mental and emotional bodybuilder, where you grow a complete set of muscles that you did not have before and you keep working on strengthening them with time. The stronger your mental and emotional muscles, the more happy and successful you become.

# 12

## JOIN THE RELAY RACE

*Nothing is particularly hard if you divide it into small jobs.*
— Henry Ford

There is a delicate and very important balance that you need to strike between planning ten years ahead and not thinking about anything else other than what you are supposed to do today. If you are spending the day thinking about all the risks and troubles that will or could unfold in the next few months, you will get pretty powerless and there is very little that you can do in a single day that can reverse or deflect things that are happening over a much longer time span.

The key lies in knowing when to zoom out and when to zoom in, when to plan and when to take action. Let's think about it this way. You have taken a step back, you've looked at the big picture, the strengths, the weaknesses, the threats, the opportunities. You analyzed, you devised a plan that will take place over a certain period of time, perhaps several months, maybe even several years. Now comes the time for action. Every day you should be concerned with the things you need to act on today only. That is where all your focus should be: what is happening today.

In an Olympic relay race, every team has four runners. The race is split into four parts where each runner runs one hundred meters and then hands over the baton to the next runner who is waiting for them at the end of their one hundred meters and so on until the race is complete, four hundred meters in total. Think about this plan that you devised like it is an Olympic relay race. Instead of four runners and four parts, think of a race divided into 365 parts by 365 runners if the plan was taking place over a year (365 days). Every day is done by one runner, so all you need to concern yourself with is your race that will finish at the end of the day. You do not need to worry about tomorrow because someone else will run that part after you hand the baton to them. You do not need to feel bad about what happened yesterday because someone else was responsible for that. All you should focus on is today. Although it is the same person biologically that will be running every day, you need to psychologically think of them as different people. Once you liberate yourself from all the worries and anxieties that tomorrow was plaguing you with and all the troubles that yesterday was crushing you with, you will sprint like a catapult. *Pouuuuf!*

Now, when tomorrow comes, it becomes today and you are a fresh, new runner in the relay who is ready to deal with it. One day at a time. This approach not only gives you laser-like focus and speed but also allows you to enjoy the day a lot more as a result of removing all the worries and negative energy that used to be associated with thinking about tomorrow or yesterday.

# 13

# YOUR TOUGHEST COMPETITOR

*The goal is not to be better than the other man,*
*but your previous self.*
— The Dalai Lama

It almost seems like we've been bred to compare what we have or what we've achieved to other people. From an early age at school, report cards are issued regularly which force us to think about how we stack up against our classmates. In sports teams, the same thing happens. Not everyone gets to play at the official games, only the best players. Also, not everyone gets equally praised by the coach, which forces you to compare how good you really are compared to everyone else. We have been conditioned since a very young age to determine how well we're doing in life by measuring ourselves against how well other people are doing and how we compare to them. That is simply wrong. This might be news to you that is arriving a little late in your life. But it is never too late to correct something.

There are many reasons why it is not right to compare your performance to other people or to determine your self-worth based on how other people are doing compared to you. The first reason is because, if we were really in a race with others, then for any race to be fair, then all the runners would have to start on the same line, at the same time. But that's not what happens in real life. Take, for example, a typical scenario in high school—the soccer team. You are so impressed by Ryan who can score goals easily, and you can't help but think about how much you suck at soccer compared to Ryan.

What you don't know is that Ryan's father is a huge soccer fan, and one of his obsessions is seeing his son grow up to be a soccer star. What you don't know as well is that Ryan's dad has hired a personal soccer coach to train Ryan three times a week. That personal coach has been a huge factor behind Ryan's impressive goal scoring capabilities. Of course, Ryan and his father never shared this with anyone to make his performance look more impressive. Is it a fair comparison now to think about how good you are at soccer compared to Ryan? Who knows where you would be if you had one-on-one private lessons with a soccer coach three times a week, offering you a customized program to improve your soccer game.

We can take another example at your typical neighborhood dance studio, where so many girls go to practice and improve their dance skills. There are always a few girls who are the stars of the studio and the envy of the rest of their colleagues. One of those is Esmerelda, a charming dancer with green eyes and blond hair, who dances so elegantly and can pick up any new move instantly. While the rest of the dancers have to practice the move many times to make it look good, Esmerelda is a natural who always gets it on the first time. Every time this happens, the rest of the girls at the studio can't help but think how clumsy they are compared to Esmeralda. In reality, they are not clumsy at all. They are all terrific dancers, but when they think about what they don't have and what Esmerelda does, it shatters their self-image.

If only the rest of the girls knew how science can explain why Esmeralda seems to be so talented and that this has nothing to do with their self-image. Esmeralda was brought into dance by her parents at the age of seven. Back then, had you met her, you would not see any of the elegance we talked about today. She was a very clumsy child. Her biomechanics greatly improved as she spent years learning to dance from a young age. When you repeat a movement many times, your body memorizes it—it's called muscle memory. You can now do this movement in your sleep. The younger you are, the easier it is. Muscle memory is also improved as the brain-body connection is improved. When your brain gives your different muscles a signal to contract in order to move your body and produce a dance move, the better the brain-body connection, the faster your body will be able to react, and the more elegant and coordinated the whole move will look. It will also improve your capacity to conduct several moves at the same time, which require different body parts to move together.

Having spent many years dancing since a young age, Esmeralda developed a very strong brain-body connection and very good muscle memory; just like a bodybuilder can grow big muscles over time. Most sophisticated dance moves are basically a combination of more basic dance moves done at different speeds in different patterns. Since Esmerelda picked up so many basic moves over her years dancing and developed such a strong brain-body connection from hours of practice, she can now easily reshuffle those moves in different combinations and patterns to create what look like new moves. This connection explains her ability to easily pick up new moves in class as the other girls need more time to master it.

Who knows, maybe all the other girls would have been better dancers than Esmerelda had they started at the same age she did and continued consistently as her parents forced her to. Maybe, given all the years Esmeralda had to practice, her level is not impressive at all, and she should have become a much better dancer. You see, things start looking very different once you keep the right context in mind. Remember that when people give an impressive performance, they don't recount all the reasons that resulted in them becoming so good at what they just did. It adds to their mystery and air of superiority when they don't share with everyone the things behind their success. They prefer to make it look effortless, like they are a natural. Which leaves you thinking about how much you suck because you can never be so natural.

There are so many other elements that make this an uneven playing field. Take genetics, for instance. Sebastien is a boxer and he inherited a naturally slim and strong body because both of his parents led a very athletic lifestyle. One of his teammates, Andrew, has to struggle with losing weight because he doesn't have the same genes that Sebastien inherited from his parents. Now Andrew has to put in so much time in activities whose sole focus is to lose weight so he won't be disqualified for being above the tournament weight class when the competition date arrives. All this extra time and energy that Andrew puts into weight loss is time that Sebastien uses to improve his technique, punching power, and other things that ultimately make him a better boxer than Andrew. Do you see where this is going? Is Sebastien really a better boxer than Andrew? Maybe if Andrew had Sebastien's weight-friendly genes he would have performed so much better than Sebastien ever dreamed of performing. Maybe he would have knocked Sebastien out! Do you see how it is completely unfair to compare the performance of one person to another? There are so many hidden parameters that you have not factored into your comparison.

It gets worse. Let's look at the role that household environments play. Let's visit Lara's house, who is a top student at her school. She is an only child, she has all the attention from her parents who are very loving and go very far to ensure that Lara is happy. Lara's classmate Mia, on the other hand, wasn't as fortunate. She has four other siblings and has to compete with them for the attention of her parents, who are not on good terms and spend most of their time at the house fighting and screaming. That environment really affects Mia and makes her sad, so she spends a lot of time alone and has trouble focusing on her studies. Where could Mia be if she was born into a different family?

The same phenomena can be seen in the world of entrepreneurship, which has become such a fashionable craft that everyone wants to be an entrepreneur. Everyone wants to come up with an idea and go and raise lots of money from investors who are willing to finance it. With startups raising money left and right, such entrepreneurs use how much money they raised as a meter stick to compare their performance and, consequently, their ability and self value to other entrepreneurs. In their eyes, there is a big difference in capability between someone who wasn't able to raise any money compared to someone who raised a little money compared to someone who raised a lot of money.

But here we go again with all the missing factors when we praise an entrepreneur called Richard who was able to raise ten million dollars fresh out of college on just an idea. Not knowing that Richard comes from a very wealthy family and although he did not take money from his family, he certainly used his family's powerful connections, many of which invested in his company or helped guide him on how to raise money or introduced him to other influential investors—all because of the good name of his family. Rebecca, on the other hand, who could have performed better than Richard, didn't get the same privilege because she comes from a poor Black community in the US, wasn't able to access the same network of investors, and for the few meetings she had, she wasn't able to project the same shining image of confidence and destined-for-greatness archetype that Richard was able to as a result of being groomed for greatness since a young age. Maybe if Rebecca had grown up in Richard's household she would have done better than him.

Comparison does not threaten our mental health alone but our financial health as well. In our adult lives we take these comparisons further. We look at the type of car that people around us are driving. If it is much nicer than ours, then we assume that they are doing much better than we are, that we are not doing well, or at least not good enough. We compare other things, such as the size of our house and the neighborhood it's in. When such comparisons make us feel inferior we might find ourselves making bad decisions, such as buying a more expensive house than we can afford or a more fancy car. Such decisions can eventually lead to our financial ruin.

Do you know that in some cultures the size of a wedding reflects the rank of the family in society. Millions of people around the world take out loans and spend money they don't have in order to finance a wedding that will be just as big as the ones they've been invited to. They do it to project a bigger image of themselves. This madness is repeated in so many different ways, but you get the point. On the business side, we talked about how entrepreneurship is currently trending and how raising money from investors is regarded as a meter stick by many entrepreneurs (and investors) on how well a startup is doing or on the performance of the entrepreneur. As a result of such comparisons, you have entrepreneurs trying to raise money from investors that they should not be raising simply because of how they would be perceived if they don't. As a result, they end up trying to push their investors to accept certain terms that they saw other startups get away with, ultimately making the whole deal fall through because it wasn't reasonable. If they were just focused on their own journey instead of others their fate could have been different.

So, we have seen plenty of examples of what not to do. What should we do instead? You should only be competing with yourself, not with anyone else. If you want to compare, make a comparison with yourself, not with other people. Compare where you are today to where you were last year or last month. This is the only comparison that matters, because it is the only comparison that is relevant and fair. There is no point in looking at how well you are doing compared to other people because you have been given things that are very different from what they have been given. While on the surface some people might look like they are doing better than you, in reality you might have accomplished much more than them because you were given a fraction of the privileges they had and you did so much more with what you were given compared to what they did.

A structured way to think about this is to ask yourself, what are the things that you want to measure? Do you want to do better financially? Is health the priority? Career progression? For each of the factors that you want to measure, you can now look at them over a period of time. First look at the big picture; where are you now compared to last year. What about five years ago?

Are you better or worse in that department? If you are doing better, make note of the reasons that led to this. If you are doing worse, ask yourself why. Was it because you weren't measuring it? Was it because it wasn't important? Or was it a priority and you were attempting to get better but you failed? If you failed, then what are the strategies that didn't work, what changes need to be made? That's the thinking process you need to apply. Remember, *it is not about winning; assholes win all the time. It is about being the best possible version of yourself. That is going way above winning.*

After you have made your high-level decisions and outlined your course of action, you need to track how you are doing in the short-term, stopping everyday to measure how you are doing in the departments you care about relative to the day before. Take note of what worked well and what didn't, slightly changing your course of action if need be to accommodate for the new data that is now available. Everything should be quantifiable. You can't improve what you don't measure—you need numbers. If you are trying to improve your sprinting, you need to be looking at your running time very closely. If it's sales you're looking to improve, then it's also your numbers that you should be monitoring. How much are you selling this week versus last week? If it's your temper that you are trying to improve, then you need to monitor how many instances happened today where you lost your temper. Did that number go up or down relative to last week or the day before? Remember that it takes time to see results. Don't expect your life to change overnight. As long as you are consistent with the effort, you will see results in due time.

That is the only way you can be strict on yourself: by comparing you to you, not to other people. Coincidentally, it also happens to be the only way you will be able to sustainably get ahead of everyone else. That is, if getting ahead even mattered in the first place. Because the only thing that matters is getting ahead of yourself.

*If people knew how hard I have to work to*
*gain my mastery, it wouldn't seem wonderful at all.*
— Michelangelo

# 14

# CONSISTENCY vs. INTENSITY

*Success is peace of mind, which is a direct result of self-satisfaction in knowing you made the effort to do your best to become the best you are capable of becoming. Ambition means tying your wellbeing to what other people say or do. Sanity means tying it to your own actions.*
— Marcus Aurelius

If you had to choose between consistency and intensity, which one do you think is more valuable? Which one would you pick? Was that your theoretical answer or is it actually what you regularly choose in your life?

We know the benefits of intensity; a strong push, a large leap, that can give you a comfortable advance. But the drawback of intensity is that it's not sustainable. You can't continue pushing with that level of intensity. Otherwise something is going to break. What usually happens when people choose intensity is that they commit to going to the gym and getting fit, they have a great first two weeks, and they go all out. They lift weights as heavy as they can, not missing a single day and maybe even doing two workouts per day. The result by the end of the second week is that they crash, whether because they are totally exhausted or because they might even have gotten injured, and then this whole activity fades away and gets forgotten. You can relate. You have done it before, whether it is going to the gym or something else.

Consistency, on the other hand, does not have the drawbacks that intensity has. If instead you chose to go to the gym three times a week for a vigorous workout instead of going every day, or if you chose to workout every day for a light twenty minutes, it is much more likely that you could continue doing this for a full year, as opposed to a meager two weeks. Big results take time to achieve. The benefits of consistency is that it produces results because consistency gives you a longer survival timespan and that's what you need to be able to produce results. As opposed to intensity, which can only last for short bursts of time, this might be suited for performance, i.e demonstrating something you already know how to do very well. But when it comes to learning, growing, and improving, intensity is not a suitable horse for the journey, for it won't make it that far.

It might seem logical now, but consistency is not how most people go about things when they set a new goal.

We learned to favor a more glorified thrust to new initiatives. Push as hard as you can, run as fast as you can, cut down on sleep. That's what we have been taught, and it is a really bad habit. For me, when it came to the choice between consistency and intensity, I used to do something much worse. I used to go for consistent intensity. I was intense not only for a short burst, I was intense all the time. I remember for my first startup straight out of college, there were no weekends—not just for me, but for everyone at the company. I used to say, what do we need a weekend from? Don't we love what we do? Isn't this what we turned down many other things for? Aren't we pursuing our dream? Weekends are for people working "jobs" they're tired of and need to get away from so they can continue doing their work the week after.

I was obviously very wrong and so naive as with many other decisions during the younger years of my life. It is endearing how juvenile passion can turn invalid justifications into philosophy. Here's what happened to the no weekend policy at my first startup. Well, after the first time we got some really bad news, I met with the team and said, let us just take the weekend off to relax. From there on, we kept the new weekends-off tradition.

Weekends do not exist for you to take a break from boring activities. They exist because no matter how passionate about your work or the activity you are engaged in, it takes a toll on your mind and body, which need rest in order to function properly. So, the work hard until you bleed culture that we glorify is very misleading. Yes, work hard, but also get plenty of rest so that you can function properly and not break anything in your mind or body that will prevent you from continuing to work hard in the future.

Looking at it from afar, intensity might look like a tiger while consistency might look like a domestic cat. The tiger seems more exciting and more useful—the animal you want on your team. Let us take a more scientific look at this. Let us see what mathematics has to say about improving. If you were to improve 1% every day, how much improvement will you have achieved after one full year of improving 1% every day? Take a minute to think about it and give me an answer. What is the number? How much would you grow if you target a minimal yet consistent 1% improvement every day? 12% improvement? 365%?

The answer is neither. The correct answer, mathematically, is 3,778.34%. That means you will improve by a phenomenal 37.78 times by the end of the year if you only commit to improving 1% every day. That is simply mind-blowing. That is the power of consistency. Which culture should be glorified now? I wish they taught this in high school. No need to scream from the top of your voice, no need to rush in. Just give 1% more every single day, don't miss a day, and watch yourself magically transform. This is very different from how we have been taught to approach things. We like to jump in, dive deep. We want that 50% improvement immediately, and when we don't get it or can't keep up with that exciting pace of improvement, our interest fades since we don't see results coming back with the same intensity that we put in.

Be aware that consistency also cuts in the opposite direction. What happens if you get worse at something by 1% every day? Perhaps due to lack of activity or practice. By the end of the year, you will have lost 97% of your level, which means you will have reached almost zero.

In summary, if we want to go further, let us make our steps smaller and let us take those steps more frequently. Consistency and discipline go hand in hand. The beauty of consistency is that it does not demand so much of us in a single day; it is something that even those who lack discipline can do. Just 1% more is not asking too much. Anyone who can't commit to that is not serious about improving to start with.

Time to go back to the drawing board, pick up the goals you were serious about, the areas you want to improve in. These might be already underway or still ideas in your head. In either case, revisit the milestones you set for yourself for each goal and divide them into smaller steps. What does 1% improvement look like tomorrow?

What does it look like for an end of week improvement? Write them down clearly, stick to them, and enjoy the guaranteed gains. It's nice to know that you don't have to suffer through everything in order to gain something.

# 15

# YOU ARE CAPABLE OF
# LEARNING ANYTHING

*Man does not simply exist but always decides what his
existence will be, what he will become the next moment.
By the same token, every human being has the freedom
to change at any instant.*
— Viktor Frankl

We have all been there before. We've tried something new only to quickly come to the conclusion that we are just not good at it. So we stop and don't try again. Even when we try again, a few years later, maybe at the insistence of someone, we come to the same conclusion. We are frustrated by the little progress we are making or by how we are struggling to do something that other people seem to do so well and so naturally, and so we stop again and we present ourselves with the same narrative. It's just not us, we decide. It is not for us. We don't know how to do it.

Some people might have felt this as they read through some of the chapters in this book. Before even giving it a shot, you might have doubted your ability to apply this framework because you find it difficult to think that way, or what it takes to apply this framework is not in your character. For example, when reading about eliminating anxiety and stress, you might have been thinking that you would never be able to do that because you are such a stress ball that it almost defines who you are. You might have been reading about the need to set healthy boundaries in relationships with your close friends and even family while thinking you could never get yourself to do that because of how close you are to these people.

You'll likely come to the same conclusion with other things that conflict with your self-image. If you have come to view yourself as a shy person, you will find it hard to try to change that. Surprisingly, the reason it is hard to change is not because of the work that needs to be done, but rather the mental obstacles that you set up in front of the work. Your mental conviction that you'll never be able to do that because it is just not you or because you suck at it. Those are the biggest reasons why you will not be able to change or adopt a new skill. To move forward, you must release the stereotypes that you have created about yourself. Because I have news for you: you can change who you are, or who you think you are.

Take me, for example. My high level of confidence has played an instrumental role in my life. Despite getting me in trouble a few times, it has served me well for the most part. People notice me talking to celebrities as if they are just some average person when I'm meeting them for the first time. Ultimately, that's what gets such celebrities to be attracted to your energy, because celebrities are used to people being starstruck, so this is how you stand out. On the romantic side, there was a time in my life where I couldn't walk into a room without walking away with the phone number of the most attractive woman in the room. I didn't care if she was standing alone or with someone, the result was the same. While that was an unhealthy condition that I ended up ridding myself of, the point here is to demonstrate the level of confidence in any circumstance.

I developed the confidence to take on any challenge, any obstacle, any opponent regardless of the difference in skill or how much the odds might be stacked against me. As a matter of fact, I don't recall the last time I did something where the odds were in my favor. I have been the underdog my whole life because I always took on challenges that are way above my punching power. I have confidence that gives me conviction that however small the chances, I will always find a way to win. So, why am I telling you this?

The explanation that comes to your mind is quite a simple one. Some people are confident, some are shy. Sherife was born super confident; it is a gift that others don't have. Well, what if I told you that you are wrong? That when I was younger, I was the shiest kid that ever lived? Today, on a scale of one to ten, I am confident ten out of ten, but when I was younger, I was shy twelve out of ten! Let me give you some examples. You got an impression that I'm a natural with women, so let us see what it was like in school.

I vividly remember a birthday party where five girls I knew, one after the other, asked me to dance, and I said no to every single one. Not because I didn't want to, but because I was so shy I couldn't get myself to say anything else. It was such a hilarious and sad scene at the same time. One girl goes up to me to ask me to dance and I say no, the rest of the girls seeing this and given the competition between girls are each thinking to themselves they are going to dance with me and tease the other girl that was turned down. So, the second girl proceeds to ask me, being confident that she will get a yes since she knows me only to get a no, and then the third, fourth, fifth, same result. I did not say no because I was being an asshole, but because it was "in my nature" to be shy. I just couldn't get myself to react in any other way!

If it was in my nature to be so extremely shy, how could I transform into the other end of the spectrum?

How could I become such a dangerously confident person? The only explanation is that it *is* possible to change who you are or who you think you are. Let me give you another example to settle any doubts you may have about how shy I really was. In high school, I fell in love with an upperclassman. She was absolutely gorgeous. I wondered how nobody managed to date her, possibly because she was just too attractive to even come near to. This girl I was fascinated with, I recall one night I ran into her in front of a night club. I was so happy about this coincidence and even ecstatic about how she seemed excited to see me. I found myself taking a short walk with her outside, only to find her confessing that she has feelings for me. I completely froze. I said something back that was actually defensive, and she asked me not to make fun of her feelings. I felt like I was driving a car that I was completely losing control of. She did all the work, supposedly made it super easy, and I struggled to say something as simple as "I love you too" or even "I like you too." I was just hilariously shy, it was embarrassing. At the end I told her I had to get back to my friends and went back to the club, and left the girl that I had been thinking about every day.

The next day at school, she came up to me again with a calm and fun composure. That was my second chance, but I couldn't get myself to do anything better this time. This pattern continued and it took me a whole semester to amass just enough courage to ask her out, when it could've been something that was so easy to do the first night she confessed her feelings. Now do you believe how shy I really was? If I could make this extreme transformation from being the shiest kid in school to the level of confidence I have now, I'm sure you are not demanding a more dramatic change with regards to the action you are struggling to take but don't find it in your nature to do.

You don't make a transformation overnight; it ultimately takes years. Every day you take a small step, over time it adds up to a journey. Demand of yourself a tiny step today in the direction that you want to go for the habit that you want to acquire or the trait you want to change. Just 1%, and another 1% the next day. That way you won't set the bar too high where you will ultimately fail and lose motivation. Be patient with yourself. These things take time. And whatever happens, remain resolute that you can change anything you want to change about yourself. Ultimately, you will find yourself avoiding environments that don't make you comfortable. But you must spend time in such environments if these are areas you want to improve in. Every day try to stick around for a little longer in such situations. You will find that with time your capacity has greatly improved. If you make mistakes, don't beat yourself up—mistakes are part of the growth process. You now know what does not work, so you have a better chance of getting it right next time.

In my senior year in high school, I was selected with a few other top students to appear on a panel to debate some international relations in front of the first lady. As a last check, all five of us were brought together the night before and asked our opinion on some political questions to see how we would perform. When my turn came, I was asked a simple question that I don't recall now. I started answering. A few seconds into it, I recall I was just saying whatever came out of my mouth and I had no answer or specific opinion that I was trying to express or a point that I was trying to make. What happened? I choked, I got nervous and I choked. I just couldn't think. That was the first time I was asked to speak at such a high profile event. Fast-forward many years and I became an international speaker in front of hundreds of high-profile guests at some of the busiest capitals that ranged from New York City, London, Paris, and Dubai. If you look on the internet you will find a video of a fundraiser in New York City that me and Fareed Zakaria, the famous journalist, were invited to as keynote speakers. There, I decided to make fun of Fareed at the opening of my speech, as he sat in the front row, given how long he went overtime with his speech before me and kept me waiting. The audience was dying from laughter. How did I get so comfortable? I would be on stage with CEOs and chairmen of companies making tens of billions of dollars in revenue, and after the event, the biggest line of people waiting to talk to one of the speakers or get their business card was the line to talk to me. How could I muster such a transformation in my public speaking skills?

Baby steps is the answer. I watched how other people did it. I noticed the things that the audience responded well to. I read books, I watched my own performance on video, and I took note of the mistakes I made. I tried to be better every time, even if just a little better—and the most important thing? I never stopped improving. I just gave you three examples from my life that debunk the "he was born with this" myth. The myth that makes you tell yourself, "I wasn't, I could never be like that." You can if you want to, you can if you are willing to practice regularly for years, and you can if you are willing to celebrate the small advances that you make and use them as motivation to make more advances.

This does not just apply to skills such as negotiation, presentation, and fundraising. This applies to more personal and delicate life skills too, such as how to create boundaries, how to not stress, etc. For these more delicate personal skills that involve your relationships with other people, you might experience some pushback from people initially. They might not like how the steps you are taking to protect your independence and well-being will ultimately reduce their influence on you and the freedom they have to infringe on your life. You must not be discouraged when you experience such resistance. The status quo is not right; it is unhealthy and there is a significant price that you are paying as a result. Keep going with the changes that you decide you want to make until you see the results that you want.

When it comes to other things in life that you can't do, remember: you don't suck at it, you just need a new skill. Identify the skill that you need to succeed in this specific endeavor, find well reviewed books on this topic, study them diligently, and find people around you whom you recognize as very good at this skill. Ask them questions, make them your unofficial mentors. Be consistent with how much you practice, and watch how much progress you will have made in a year. Remember that the most important element for change or progress is time. You have to give it enough attention and time. If you are not making enough progress on a new skill, then you must give it more time and attention, instead of losing hope and giving less.

# 16

## YOU ARE SHRINKING YOUR CIRCLE OF INFLUENCE

*In life our first job is this, to divide and distinguish things into two categories: externals I cannot control but the choices I make with regard to them I do control. Where will I find good and bad? In me, in my choices.*

— Epictetus

We spend so much time thinking about all the things that concern us. The economy, the weather, wars, injustice, etc. Little do we know, that most of this thinking does not just stress us out and make us anxious but it diminishes the power we have over the things we are thinking about. We must consciously channel our thinking into a direction that will instead increase our power over the large array of things that concern us. To do that, we must first understand the difference between our circle of concern and our circle of influence.

Everything in our life can be divided into one of those two circles. If it is something that we care about and can alter or change its trajectory, then it belongs in our circle of influence. If it is something that we care about but it is far from our control, then it belongs in our circle of concern. Our circle of concern is far bigger than our circle of influence. We care about and are interested in a lot more things than what we can control or change.

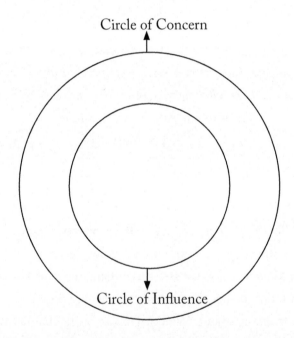

Illustration #1: Our circle of concern is much larger than our circle of influence

Thinking about how one of our loved ones has been diagnosed with cancer and how we wish that they will be cured from it is in our circle of concern. We have no direct control over the cancer; we can't prevent it from multiplying or spreading to other areas of the body. The more we think about this situation and how it makes us sad, the more it kills our morale and renders us helpless to do anything to help them while also reducing our productivity in other areas of our life.

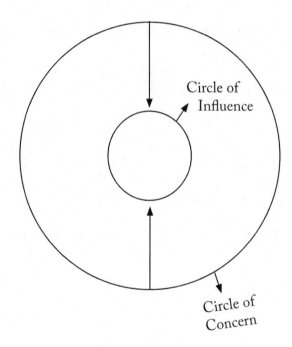

Illustration #2: What happens when we focus on our circle of concern?

On the same topic, what could lie in our circle of influence? Spending time with our loved one who has cancer, cheering them up, and making sure they are in high spirits and have enough positive energy to increase the chance that their body will respond positively to the cancer treatment. We could also research alternative treatments, a new diet for them to try, etc. Those are certainly things we could do. With this shift in thinking, we have suddenly increased our circle of influence. We are actually able to improve the chances that they will recover by focusing on the things we can alter.

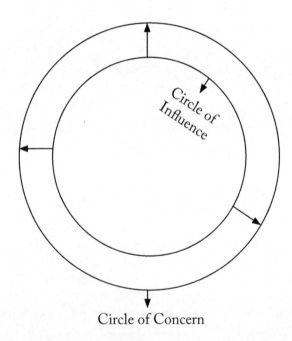

Circle of Concern

Illustration #3: What happens when we focus on our circle of influence?

When we focus on our circle of concern, our circle of influence shrinks. When we focus on our circle of influence instead, it grows. We must be constantly conscious of our thoughts, always separating them into one of these two circles. If we catch ourselves worried about something in our circle of concern, we must think about the closest derivative to it that belongs in our circle of influence. When we focus on our circle of influence, not only do we have a higher chance of achieving the outcome we hope for but we also feel much stronger, effective, and in control.

If you missed a train or a flight for a meeting, the immediate trap is taking a slide down your circle of concern and worrying about all the things that could go wrong as a result, which you can't control. Or you could focus on your circle of influence and instead find the next flight or train you can realistically get on, inform the people you are meeting with accordingly, and spend this time preparing for the meeting as opposed to behaving erratically which will drastically affect your performance at the meeting once you arrive.

# PART III

## THE ROAD LESS TRAVELED

# 17

## IF YOU EXPECT LIFE TO BE PAIN-FREE, YOU WILL SUFFER

*We lost because we told ourselves we lost.*
— Leo Tolstoy

There is the old rhetorical question that asks whether you look at life as a glass half full or half empty. Is life full of pain or full of beauty? Anyone, no matter their age, will have experienced their share of both beauty and pain by the time they have completed their life. How we live our life determines which of the two represents the lion's share of our life. If you were to diligently apply all the frameworks outlined in this book, you should be able to experience a lot more beauty than pain. Not because you were magically transported to another planet that lacks anything harmful. But because you have developed a strong immunity, even when you're exposed to harmful and dangerous pathogens they are not able to inflict the intended harm on you. The frameworks you have learned here can help disarm the pain that was supposed to be inflicted on you from the events that were intended to hurt you.

We have learned in previous chapters that setting expectations is a recipe for disappointment (see chapter 1). It is just as true when we expect life to be pain-free. We were raised to expect that life should be carefree and happy. That it is only in exceptional times and events where we will experience pain. When something bad happens it should be a rare occurrence. This is a big departure from reality. Look at the world around us: it is torn by war, conflict, disease, injustice, and hypocrisy. Let us recognize life for what it is—there is plenty of pain and suffering. The only antidote to it is in how we deal with harm when it comes our way. How do we strip it from its sting?

There is peace in knowing that pain is coming. If it cannot be avoided, we can be consoled knowing that after pain comes healing. Pain is a great instructor; it is the process of our brain and body updating out-of-date information that resulted in pain making its way into our life. Pain is an opportunity for growth, to develop our immune system so that next time pathogens enter our environment we are able to identify them and weed them out before they can harm us again.

Life can be painful; when we expect it to be pain-free, we suffer mentally. So, let us not expect it to be pain-free.

That way, when it actually becomes pain-free, we rejoice, we can be grateful. When pain arrives we are not surprised, for we expected it. We are able to greatly reduce the painful effect of something just by expecting it to happen.

It is chasing the perfect life that makes the journey so painful, because we experience so many imperfections along the way. The perfect life does not exist; it is an illusion. You sometimes think if you could amass enough wealth and power you could give yourself a happy life and shelter yourself from all the pain. Well, let us look at celebrities. Why do so many of them commit suicide if that assumption were true? Even if we go to the hallways of power, to kings and dictators, all the influence they consolidated was not able to bring them peace. Instead, their minds are full of suspicion of internal and external threats to their power. Everybody is suffering from something. Everyone at all economic levels. There is no level of wealth or power that can shelter you from suffering—the only thing that can is your mind.

The perfect life only exists in being content with what you have, even if all that you have is suffering and misery. Let's define suffering. Is it going through unpleasant situations and experiencing unpleasant events or is it feeling pain? Or both? We need to differentiate between the two because, in a way, you can suffer without suffering. It may be hard for you to control whether you experience unpleasant events. We cannot control that the bus we got on has an accident that inflicts severe physical damage on us. We cannot control that a loved one dies or experiences a sudden unexplained terminal illness. While we might have more control on people, we still cannot fully control how people treat us or what they choose to think of us.

But let me tell you what you can surely control: how you react to such unfortunate events. The only healthy way to react to them is almost with a sense of indifference. That is how you can strip harmful events from their sting. You can't prevent the events from happening but you can prevent them from turning you into a sour and miserable person. I clearly recall the most difficult time in my life, the time I experienced too many perfect storms. Multiple extremely unlikely catastrophic events, whose probability of happening at the same time was close to zero, yet happen they did. When all these events happened at the same time, that destroyed many areas of my life and almost destroyed my life as a whole. It was that same time where I also happened to be the happiest in my life. How was that possible?

Was I happy because of these tragic events? No. I am simply highlighting that experiencing a catastrophe (or catastrophes in my case) and feeling very happy are two things that can coexist. That point in my history was where I actually learned this framework. When the bad news started to come, I was very upset, furious. What did I do to deserve this? I should be rewarded, not punished! As the bad news kept coming, so did my disbelief. Is this really happening? It was a very difficult time at first. Until I learned that suffering is optional.

We can experience dreadful events, but we don't have to suffer through them. It is when I learned that the only thing I have left is my well-being, my health is still good, I thought, and I haven't lost my mind just yet. I can't afford to lose those as well. I must guard them at all costs.

From that point on, it was like splitting the land. On one side I needed to rationally deal with the events that unfolded and dig my way out of them. On the other hand, I couldn't feel negatively about them. Instead, I learned to indulge in as many enjoyable activities as I could to prevent me from sinking into melancholy. Such activities included sports, spending time in nature, travel when my schedule allowed, and other things. This is also why the vast majority of people I knew never realized or even felt that I was going through a hard time, let alone the biggest catastrophe of my life! Not because I was faking it, but because I was actually happy and there were no bad symptoms that people could observe. I did not let the bad events infect my spirit. This was something I had to evolve into. Again, I was not born like that, and I did not capture this spirit overnight.

This experience was not due to my superhuman abilities; I am not superhuman. I am human. It was due to me conceptualizing and adopting this framework of thinking that I outlined. That means you and everyone else can do the same. It would be such a waste of life if you don't. Just give it time and practice. I was devastated at first until I learned how I should deal with such situations. Remember: when you are happy, you are not happy *because*, you are happy *despite*.

*What matters to an active man is to do the right thing;*
*whether the right thing comes to pass should not bother him.*
— Goethe

# 18

# YOUR INVISIBLE EGO IS DESTROYING YOU

*The first principle is that you must not fool yourself,*
*and you are the easiest person to fool.*
— Richard Feynman

*Ego* (noun): A person's sense of self-esteem or self-importance

The first thing you told yourself when you read the title of this chapter was probably "I don't have an ego" or "I used to have an ego but I don't have one anymore. I should probably skip this chapter." Which is the reason why you should read this chapter very carefully. Your ego is alive and strong. It is alert to every threat to its existence and will actively trick you and divert your attention away from anything that might rid you of it.

When we hear the word "ego" we usually clear ourselves from any claims that we might have one, partly because we don't understand well what the ego is. We usually think of someone who has an ego as an arrogant person who is snobbish and rude. You can see their ego walking in front of them as they walk into the room. While that is indeed the ego at play, that is a scaled up version of the ego that is very easy to spot. The ego we are going to discuss here, however, is much more subtle and is present in every single person, inflicting self-damage on us without us even being aware of its existence.

Your ego is not your amigo. In fact, it is your biggest enemy. It is the biggest force of self-destruction that is active in your life. It has already caused you so many problems with people, strained many relationships, and ended some. It has overextended you into committing to things beyond your current capabilities or resources, causing you only pain and damage in the process. The most dangerous thing about ego is that it is like carbon monoxide, an invisible poisonous gas that has no odor, which makes it very hard to detect. Carbon monoxide is a threat to every household that has a heater running on gas. In a similar way, ego is a threat to every person.

The problem with ego is that it will make you think that you have gotten rid of it, that you don't have an ego anymore. But ego is like an iceberg, the part you might have gotten rid of is the part above sea level, the obvious part, the one you can easily see. But if you were to realize the giant that exists under the sea, that affects every area of your life without you realizing, you would be astonished.

## They did it to me

When things go wrong, when you fail at a project that you embarked on, the first thing to point fingers at is usually the circumstances, the bad economy, people letting you down, the weather, basically anything but you. That is your ego again, active in full force.

What the ego does here is strip you from the opportunity to actually learn from your mistakes. It does this by deflecting the blame for failure far away from you, putting it on external factors you had no control over. When this happens, you believe there is no need to change how you make decisions or even look into old habits or character traits that you need to get rid of. As a result, the ego primes you for a second and third failure whenever you are ready to take the next steps because you haven't fully processed and internalized the lessons from your first failure correctly.

Stay mentally sober and be very careful of the story that you tell yourself. Your ego will usually craft a story behind what happens, and it won't be one that reflects what actually happened but one that is designed to not compromise your abilities or ethics and instead find other people and things to blame for what happened. Be very skeptical of the story you tell yourself. Lying to others is bad, but few things are more damaging than lying to yourself. What makes the ego even more dangerous is that it conceals the fact that you are lying to yourself.

### I can do that!

You had some success in your career, and your interests have grown to be beyond the field that you succeeded in. You suddenly get very excited about a field you don't have much experience in. But you don't need experience, you think, you have other things that make up for it. With your intelligence and speed, you will quickly be able to learn and succeed in this new field. Your skills are transferable to whatever area of life you set your eyes on.

That was your ego doing the talking in your head; it wasn't you. You believed it and that is why you failed. Whenever you pick a goal that is bigger than your current level of capability, you are most likely going to fail. Your ego distorts your assessment of your current level of capability, always painting an exaggerated picture of the situation.

Without your ego, instead of fully diving into this new field, you would have spent enough time developing the new skills and knowledge needed and getting some experience. You would've given yourself whatever time you needed to get ready for this new challenge, as opposed to jumping into it immediately, armed with nothing much besides your ego and its inflated assessment of everything you accomplished in life before, which does not have much relevance to this new challenge. But your ego will tell you otherwise, of course.

Instead of rushing into new commitments, projects, responsibilities, and actions, reflect on the magnitude of what you are about to embark on. Think of all the worst-case scenarios of how this could end up and prepare contingency plans for how to avoid such scenarios. What will you do if you end up in one of those worst-case scenarios?

### Touchy

If you find that you are often sensitive to the level of correctness that people treat you with and easily take offense, that is your ego alive and tripping. Ego makes you take everything personally. If you called someone and they forgot to call you back, you take that disrespectfully. Maybe they have a bad memory and are generally disorganized. Perhaps they have been wanting to call you back but they keep getting drowned into more urgent matters. Your ego will have none of that—it is disrespectful, period. I am not something that can be forgotten, it says. Such an attitude will end up straining so many relationships unnecessarily.

Ego is like a weed. You can't clean the garden of it once and say you got rid of it. You have to clean regularly, every week, maybe even every day, otherwise it will grow again. To explain most of your failures in life, whether in your professional or personal life, look no further than the guilty role that your ego played. You were not aware of it back then. Now that you are, do yourself a favor and eliminate the self-destructive role that ego plays in your life. You work too hard to let such a stumbling block that is totally within your control prevent you from having the success you truly deserve.

# 19

# LEVERAGE THE POWER OF EMPATHY

*We'd forgive most things if we knew the facts.*
— Graham Greene

*Empathy* (noun): the ability to understand and share the feelings of another

Empathy is a word that is not frequently used. Certainly not as frequently as it should be. Empathy can be described as the capacity to understand or feel what another person is experiencing from within their frame of reference. That is, the capacity to place oneself in another person's position. In situations where we must show empathy, at best, people usually show sympathy, which is very different from empathy. Sympathy is more of a feeling of pity for another. Empathy is being able to comprehend what someone is going through. Sympathy, on the other hand, is more like a feeling of relief that we are not going through the same thing.

Situations similar to the following happen on a daily basis. The supermarket cashier who isn't rude but he's also not nice. He just always seems down, gloomy, and antisocial. Sympathy recognizes his mood and rejoices that we don't feel the same way. Empathy connects with the various reasons that could force the man to be like that. Perhaps he hates his life; he is being crushed with challenges and tragedies that has made him desperate with regards to finding a way out of them. Lack of sympathy and empathy gets us to label the man as rude and full of negative energy.

This doesn't just happen with strangers in the supermarket. It happens with the closest people in our personal life and our coworkers. Take a father who is used to beating his children. Our first reaction is usually to label him as a monster who should be locked up in prison. While I am completely against the use of violence with children and in no way endorsing such behavior, perhaps the father is a victim as well. Perhaps he used to get beaten up by his own father when he was growing up and was conditioned by his old man that this is the only way to instill discipline in your children.

With this empathetic perspective, as a child receiving the beating, you no longer feel bitter about your father. You feel sorry, but you understand that he does not hate you, that out of all the unlikely places in the world, the beating actually might come from a place of love and care. Again, I am in no way endorsing this behavior, but I can empathize with it. Which is the starting point to repairing any relationship or solving any problem. Because there is no way you can do that if you don't have a proper fundamental understanding of the underlying cause of a problem. And there is no way you are going to arrive at that without empathy.

## Empathy is healthy

When someone treats you badly, you won't feel angry or upset about it if you have adopted an empathetic vision. With empathy, you can see behind the curtain of their actions, that their intention is not necessarily to harm you, that their circumstances can explain why they are behaving like that. While this does not excuse their behavior, it explains it. Now that you understand their behavior, you won't wait for people to make it up to you for you to feel at peace. You are already at peace because you understand why, because you can empathize.

Empathy is healthy because it makes you feel stronger, both mentally and emotionally. Instead of rushing to react to people's bad behavior, instead of sprinting to make them pay for it. You are able to look behind those actions and analyze. You take pride in being stronger than them, in your superior ability to manage your emotions, but you don't rub it in their face.

## Connection

Practicing empathy gives us an opportunity to connect with people on a much deeper level. To feel what they are going through, to forgive, to practice humanity. To look deeper than how they behave at the surface, to understand their circumstances. Empathy ultimately allows us to see and understand people's behavior in 3D.

Can you imagine the kind of world we would live in if most people practiced empathy? There would be no wars, no hate crimes, no racism or discrimination. People would be much happier because they are getting less upset about their immediate environment. Ghandi said, "Be the change you wish to see in the world." Practice empathy then.

It is important to realize that people have different value systems. The values that you believe are superior and most important are not the same values that other people rank the highest. For instance, you might believe that punctuality is the most important factor that determines how much you respect a person. Someone else might feel that the focus and attention you give to a person when you are with them is the best way to determine how much you respect a person. One person might feel being generous with your money is very important, and another thinks that being generous with your time and emotions is more important.

The first building block of adopting empathetic vision is to realize that everyone has a different value system. Instead of rushing to judge how people behave based on your own value system, get to know their value system first. Every person is made up of a unique DNA sequence that is not shared by two people. They were born different, and then each person proceeded to go through a very unique set of events and circumstances as they grew up that impacted their thoughts, character, and beliefs differently. All these went into creating a value system that is quite different from one person to another.

We are usually guilty of attribution bias when we see other people making a mistake. That means we give different explanations when other people make a mistake as compared to the explanation we give when we make the same mistake. When others make a mistake we blame it on a character flaw that they have. When we make the same mistake, however, we tend to obviously blame the circumstances that led us to end up here. With empathetic vision, you will learn to give people the same benefit of the doubt that you always give yourself.

## Attraction

The thing that people lack most today is being under-stood by others. If you are able to fill people with a sense that you actually understand what they are going through, you will stand out like a lighthouse. They will appreciate you and find it very hard to go far from your orbit because you provide them with something that very few others are capable of.

When you actually listen to people, it has a huge seductive effect on them. In a conversation, most people can't wait for the other person to finish talking for them to jump in and share their opinion. As a matter of fact, while the other person is talking, instead of listening, they are actually thinking about what they are going to say back. When people feel that you are genuinely listening to what they have to say it has a very powerful effect. One way to make people really feel that you have been listening to them is to repeat something that they said earlier in the conversation.

It is a very simple technique, but you can't imagine how powerful of an effect it has on people when they realize that you were not only listening but you also remember! You want to be careful not to overdo this so you don't come across as not being genuine. Another way to do this technique is to complete something they haven't said, not necessarily interrupting them to complete their sentence, but rather adding a piece of information that they have not mentioned but having listened so attentively to the whole story you can tell that this additional piece must be true as well.

## Advancement

When you practice empathy, you establish a capacity to read the person in front of you, to be conscious not just of their words and actions but their moods, thoughts, and motivations. Developing such a wide lens equips you with the capability to see through people and anticipate their actions. When you can anticipate their actions you have more time to prepare for the most suitable reaction that is bound to neutralize their advance and lower their resistance. As a result you are always one step ahead. Such skills are so crucial in the workplace that without them it will be very hard to advance ahead.

It is crucial to treat each person differently depending on their different psychology. We already established that everyone has a different value system, genetics, and upbringing. Consequently, people respond differently to the same stimulant. Some are more sensitive than others; people differ in their level of suspicion, curiosity, friendliness, etc. You need to be conscious of people's nature and deal with them accordingly as opposed to establishing some universal metric of what is right and how everyone should be and holding everyone to that standard.

Before trying to determine people's character, be aware that due to your past experience, you are bound to have natural biases that make you ignorant to knowing who people really are, and as a result it is likely you will judge people incorrectly. Your new empathetic vision will force you to broaden your view and expand your creative energy and willingness to consider other possibilities for what the people in front of you might be really like. Empathy will make you more creative and more intelligent, making your mind work in different dimensions.

## Ego

Our ego is usually the biggest obstacle between us and our ability to practice empathy. We are mostly focused inward, too conscious of the special treatment we expect from people so that we can reinforce the special self-image we have of ourselves. Once anyone treats us in a way that falls below that level of expectation, our attention is immediately turned inward to the special self-image that has been poked at by this behavior that does not conform to or validate our self-image. It is our ego that forces us to look inward. Instead, we should be focused outward, thinking about the person in front of us and what could have led them to take such actions or say such things.

People are like the sea—a whole different world that is waiting to be discovered where everyone is almost like a different creature. Turning our attention outward instead of inward to discover this different world is another muscle that we learn to grow. It takes time, but as we practice it consistently it will soon become the norm of how we look at things and perceive them. Once you get a grip of this new muscle and its importance, you will awaken to new social possibilities that you never realized existed.

The more self-love, resilience, and inner strength you have, the easier you will find it to focus your attention outward and develop empathetic vision. If you are struggling to show and practice empathy, that is a sign that you lack self-love and that your ego has too strong of a grip on you and is forcing you to look inward, making it difficult for you to turn your attention outward to other people. The Bible is full of so many verses and instructions about loving your enemy. That is possibly the epitome of empathy, and it is only for those with the most inner strength, self compassion, and self-love. Only someone that has established so much peace with their inner self can reach the freedom to venture so far outward with their empathy, to the point of loving their enemies.

*I do not ask the wounded person how he feels.*
*I myself become the wounded person*
— Walt Whitman

# 20

# WHEN SOMETHING BOTHERS YOU, SIT WITH IT

*Don't let the force of an impression when it first hit you*
*knock you off your feet; just say to it: hold on a moment; let*
*me see who you are and what you represent.*
*Let me put you to the test.*
— Epictetus

Humans are constantly stimulated in today's age. We are continuously bombarded with information and exposed to people through different mediums that include real life, phone, and television. All of this leaves a mark on us, affecting us in different ways. As it accumulates, it ultimately affects our mood, for better or worse.

In this age of constant exposure, it is hard to realize how we truly feel. Is this joy that we sense just something on the surface, below which lies a mountain of anxiety?

Or is it a deep and true joy? It is easy to take the wrong cue from how we feel, because we are not truly in touch with how we genuinely feel, but rather how it seems we feel. For instance, going from one party to another because we feel like we are excited, whereas in reality our body is drained and we should rest, but the excitement hides the fatigue.

We do not spend as much time with ourselves today so we can be self-aware and conscious of how we truly feel and what's going through our mind. Even the time that we might spend alone at home, we are not sharing it with ourselves. We spend it on our phone, on TV, procrastinating, doing anything but being in touch with ourselves, our thoughts, and our feelings. In order to comb through what lies beneath the surface, while everything seems to be going well above.

Over the years, this buildup leads to a disconnect between our conscious mind and our subconscious mind. Everything that we have swept under the carpet, that we did not take the time to process, reflect on, study, or analyze has been stored in our subconscious mind. On a daily basis, many decisions are made by our subconscious mind. We might not be able to explain why we came to these decisions or took those actions—we might even blame them on impulses. But it is actually the subconscious mind and everything that has been stored in it over many years that is now running like a software which you don't control, and maybe even worse, you are not even aware of the role that it plays in your life.

The subconscious mind is like a locked treasure that you haven't learned to access and might not even know that it exists. Some people are more aware and better trained than others to be well connected to their subconscious mind and benefit from the harmony and peace that results from this connection. The good news is that you can also access this harmony, with time. You need to build a habit of listening to yourself, to get away from all the noise so that you can hear the most important voice clearly, the voice within you. It is hard to do that when you are surrounded by people or other background noise like content on your phone or TV. You need to spend more time with yourself, listening to yourself and the thoughts and feelings that are hiding underneath.

There is someone in my life that has been very special to me since I met her during my freshman year in college. There is no doubt about how much she cares about me and loves me. It goes to an extent that she actually feels responsible for me. Her name is Isabella. I have a photographic memory of the day I was awakened to this powerful phenomenon that I didn't know existed. It was a few years ago, but I recall exactly where I was and where I was sitting. I was having a normal day, a good day. Suddenly, I recall that my mood fell off the cliff. Out of nowhere, I couldn't explain why, I suddenly began to feel really bad. I was upset, in a really bad mood. But why? No idea.

It bothered me so much that I couldn't explain this. I thought about what happened that day. Did I get any bad news? Did someone treat me badly? No. What was it then? I couldn't explain it. A few months later, the exact thing happened. This time, there was one common incident between those two days. One that was clearly not responsible for my sudden gloomy mood. I had a phone call with Isabella on both days. She unquestionably had nothing to do with my bad mood. How could someone who has never shown me anything but love and care be the one who sends my spirit into the abyss every time I talk to them?

Until the evidence for this became clear. Every time I spoke to Isabella on the phone, I felt like shit afterwards. It was hard to detect the patterns because we only spoke once every few months and we only harbored love for each other, never having any bad history. The problem was that Isabella thought very highly of me. Anything that I accomplished was a small fraction in her eyes compared to what I was truly capable of. Her expectations of me only grew bigger and more stubborn with time, and I could not keep up with them. All of this was stored in my subconscious mind. She came from a very wealthy European family, both of her parents were descendants of European royalty. My analysis was that she subconsciously used to compare me to her father and her uncles' accomplishments. She thought I was more talented than them and thus was subconsciously frustrated by how I hadn't managed to be more accomplished than them yet despite my talents.

So apparently, every time we spoke on the phone, my subconscious mind would feel like I had not achieved enough in life, that I had squandered my talent, that I was so far from fulfilling my potential there was nowhere to start. My conscious mind, on the other hand, felt the complete opposite—I had done a lot, I had come a long way, I was extremely impressive. Every call with Isabella ignited this conflict between my conscious and subconscious mind, the end result of which was my mood sinking to the bottom and having no explanation whatsoever for my sudden change of mood.

This is one short example from my life. There is plenty going on in mine and yours as well. There are times when we also feel good and attribute it to the wrong reasons without realizing it. Scan your mind anytime you feel bad. It is easy to blame your mood on trivial things like the traffic or the hot weather. You might be relieved to find a logical explanation so you don't have to exert additional effort looking for the real culprit. Sometimes the real reason you might be in a bad mood is because you haven't been sleeping well or eating a clean diet. These are two factors that are essential for our mood and well-being. Like we discussed though, don't settle for these two reasons, keep looking deeper for a bigger cause.

Once you start scanning and you hit the superficial layer of reasons, such as the traffic and weather, keep scanning deeper. If it was truly the weather and traffic behind your bad mood, there is more homework for you. If we can't change the traffic and the weather, then what is the point of being upset about them? Back to the scan, make note of when exactly you started detecting the bad mood. Did it happen suddenly or gradually? List everything that happened in between. Take note of the suspects, but don't rule anything out. As the event is repeated, look for the common denominator; is there a repeating pattern? Is there something on the list that is usually present whenever you descend into a bad mood? Great, you identified your target. Now the interesting work begins.

The target you identified might be the last suspect on your mind. It could be something as harmless as your mother, or it could be a favorite food or drink. But it is these harmless suspects that are usually behind such unlikely triggers, because they are the last thing you would expect. Now let's dig further. What is it about your mother or the target you identified that could have triggered you? Could it have to do with not being able to set healthy boundaries between each other? Is she intervening in your life too much? Once you get to the bottom of it, now you are aware of the trigger and the reason why it triggers you. You now need to resolve it and make peace with it so that it does not trigger you in the future. Making peace with the trigger is a gradual process, like most things that trouble us. To make complete peace with the trigger, you will need your empathetic vision (see chapter 19).

Here's what you need to do: every time you encounter the same situation, try to last a little longer than last time without getting triggered or upset. This process is like increasing the time you can spend underwater by expanding your lung capacity. You are not going to make a huge leap of progress in one go. Instead, you need to focus on going a little further every time, remembering the role that this stimulus has in ruining your mood and not giving it the privilege to do that. As you look back, you will find that you are able to manage the trigger slightly better every time. It is a game of inches. Soon, it will have almost no effect on you anymore.

# 21

# TURN THE BAD INTO GOOD

*My formula for human greatness is amor fati: that one*
*wants nothing to be different, not in the future, not in the*
*past, not for all eternity. Not merely to bear*
*what is necessary, but to love it.*
— Friedrich Nietzsche

We cannot control when bad things happen to us. We can only control how we react to them. In our reaction lies a range of options as wide as the difference between night and day. When we react, we have the power to recognize the bad we just experienced as the worst thing that happened to us or transform it into the best thing that happened to us. Here we realize something very profound. That we have this magical ability to shape our own lives and our destinies. The ability to shape our destiny comes from our ability to shape our vision. Change what you see and the world around you changes, and your life will change along with it.

The power accompanying this realization is unimagi-
nable. It means that there is no series of bad events,
calamities, betrayals, catastrophes, or crises that can
change our destiny. All of these are *actions*, yet it is in our
*reaction* where our life and destiny is shaped. This should
fill us with a sense of relief and peace, because we know
that we have no control over the external events that
happen in our life. All we can do is wish for good weather.
If our lives were truly determined by these external events,
we would have a much more sad and mundane reality.
We would be like a kite dancing in the wind, without
much character or personality other than what the wind
bestows upon us. History is full of examples of great
individuals who managed to lead exemplary lives and
become idols as a result of this realization.

In the fifteenth century, every reputable artist in
Renaissance Florence was sent to Rome by Lorenzo
de' Medici (de' Medici was one of the most influential
families in Florence) to work on the Sistine Chapel,
except for one: Leonardo da Vinci. This obviously was a
huge setback for Leonardo. He had never gotten along
with Lorenzo and the wealthy businessman took this
as an opportunity to rebuff him. Unfairly prevented
from engaging in the biggest artistic endeavor of his
time, Leonardo had two choices. The first was to make
a scene, to be bitter, to go into a depression and let this
event affect his artistic prowess. The second was to pursue

this goal further, to make his way to the Pope himself in Rome, to establish his credentials as a skilled artist and demand that he be given part of the work to be done on the Sistine Chapel.

What Leonardo did was a third choice. He realized that this whole patron model in Florence where a rich family commissioned you to develop a specific art of work was too limiting for his ambitions and made him too dependent on these patrons. Instead, he interpreted this setback as a much needed wake-up call, and he packed up and moved to Milan, where he created a new model for financing his artistic and scientific pursuits that was much more suitable to his individual needs and interests.

Leonardo did this by working as an advisor to powerful figures across all his areas of expertise, including but not limited to science, military machinery, and art. Instead of living for one art commission after another, he was now a year-round advisor on several fields where he enjoyed the interdisciplinary work and thinking that came about as a result.

We need to redefine some terminologies. As far as what happens to you in life, there is no good or bad. There is only good and hidden good. The hidden good are things that happen to us which seem so obviously bad on the outside but are actually gifts if we manage to take them in and make use of them. Let us imagine that you got fired from your job unfairly after all you gave and sacrificed to your company. You have the same two choices Leonardo had. The first is to go into a depression, to start a whirlpool of negativity that will ultimately drown your career. Or the second choice: to protest, to resist, to not leave without a fight, to take them to court and fight it out with all your energy for as long as it takes.

But there is the third option as well. To see the situation as a gift, the push you needed to start your own company that you have been dreaming about for years but could never get around to because you were too comfortable at that job. Without being fired, you would have never started pursuing your real dream. We do control our destiny—by controlling our perception and our reaction. Only we can choose the roads we decide to walk on, or even better, the roads we decide to pave.

There will be difficult days. We might feel pain. But it makes all the difference in the world knowing that the bad taste in our mouth is medicine that will improve us as opposed to poison that is killing us. Just the mere thought of how we interpret the events around us can kill us or take us to new heights. We shape the reality we live in through the way we interpret events and the course of action we choose to chart in response to these events. Every action that happens to us has a reaction that suits it best, one that is designed to unbox the hidden good and use it to propel our lives to new heights.

## Eliminating the ego

If you are at a stage where your ego hasn't been fully downsized yet, it is necessary to step out of your own shoes and replay the events that happened as if they had happened to someone else and have nothing to do with you. When you do that you might realize that you have exaggerated the situation and are overreacting, because it's no big deal had this happened to someone else. What the ego does is inflame the situation. It screams, "How could they do this to me?" like it is OK for this to happen to someone else, but it is not OK that it happened to me.

Now that you have eliminated the ego, you can measure the events more accurately for what they truly are. Your initial reaction might have been to leave because the ego is imploring you to do that, but once you look at things objectively by imagining that it happened to someone else, you realize that leaving is not the right course of action. Or it could be the opposite. Your initial reaction might have been to continue your commitment to something that has been absolutely draining you, but when you step out of your own shoes, you realize it's time to call it quits, to stop the bleeding and reassess the situation from the outside.

I recall when I was going through the most emotionally painful time in my life, stepping out of my shoes and releasing the ego was what kickstarted the healing process. I was in London, and a very good friend of mine became worried about how I was not recovering as quickly as they expected. I really took those events to heart and was suffering badly. He started recommending that I do a medical psychedelic treatment with a drug called psilocybin. This is the same commercial drug known as magic mushrooms. My friend was leading a new biotech company that at the time was attempting to bring the benefits of the drug into a safe clinical environment where people can have a clinic-like experience when taking the drug under supervision. He started talking to me about the benefits and the vast scientific literature backing it up.

I was in so much pain at the time, and it was the first instant in my entire life that I was thinking of taking drugs. I have never done any form of drugs before and I'm glad that I went through that painful experience because it made me empathize with many people that do drugs. Some of them are just in so much pain, they are looking for any outlet that can relieve them from this mental pain, even if it's just for a few hours. Unfortunately, many people end up resorting to commercial unsafe drugs because they do not have access to the right guidance or a more healthy environment that can encourage them to heal in a sustainable manner.

My friend explained to me that the way psilocybin works is it completely eliminates the ego from your brain. It allows you to replay the events that you experienced by seeing them as an outsider, as if they happened to someone else. When he explained to me how the drug works, I was able to replicate in my brain this process without taking the drug. I vividly recall that it was only then that the healing process started. You can benefit from a similar effect by replaying the events that happened to you and imagine that they happened to someone else. Your observations and conclusions might be entirely different, and the course of action you plan will be much better suited for your best interests when you have taken the ego out of the equation.

## Practicing objectivity

There is a framework to turning the bad into good. It starts with practicing objectivity. In order to properly interpret the meaning and effect of the events around us—to discover the golden path that will take us from the bad to the good—we must not fall victim to our subjective senses. It is because of the lack of objectivity that most people drown in negative events as opposed to realizing those events as springboards instead.

When something bad happens to us there is often a lesson that needs to be learned. Are we running around in so many circles in our life that we need what lawyers call an "act of god" in order to force us to stop what we are doing and reconsider our direction in life? In failure, did we underestimate the task, or did we overestimate our capabilities? In such events, there is always something to be learned about the world around us or about ourselves. That learning experience is crucial, otherwise we might find ourselves experiencing the same tragedy again or experiencing the same feeling we had from the first tragedy replicated in a completely different tragedy in the future.

Sometimes we are on the wrong path, yet we are completely convinced that we are doing the right thing and nobody can change our mind about that. The only way to prevent us from taking further steps in the wrong direction is such a calamity. Something forcing us to go off-road. Unfortunately, after many people experience such an event, they can't wait to fix the damage so they can get back to doing exactly what life was trying to prevent them from! So we must take the time to reflect whenever we are hit with a calamity. What message is life sending me here? This is too big to be just a coincidence.

When it comes to people, we tend to attach pretty quickly once we fall in love with someone or even meet a new friend that we feel we have so much in common with. We sometimes fill in a lot of gaps and imagine that this is the person meant for us to spend the rest of our lives with. When things go badly, it becomes very hard for us to recover because the reality we outlined in our head was shattered. Many people that come into our lives are just meant to teach us something, or to help us realize something about ourselves we were not conscious of. They are meant to play a phase in our life, a short-term role and purpose. We need to remember this when such relationships end badly, because it becomes much more painful to recover when we are still in wishful thinking mode about how it was supposed to last forever and we start idealizing how great it was. If we are wearing our objective lens, we will realize that if it really was that great, we wouldn't have been in the situation we are suffering from now.

Pain has been recently glorified by our society. There are plenty of motivational videos glamorizing how you should embrace pain and how it is the only pathway to success. I disagree with this fad. Pain is a sign that you are doing something wrong, that you need to stop and reconsider the path you are on. It is especially true for relationships with people. Romantic relationships do not need to be painful—challenging, OK, but not painful. If someone is causing you pain regularly, this is a clear sign that you need to fundamentally change your relationship with them or abort it completely.

If you are experiencing severe pain during a workout, that is a sign that you are probably about to tear a muscle or inflict some serious damage on yourself. Pain is a biological signal that tells you to stop. It is designed to protect you from harm. What we need is a little bit of discomfort in our lives to make sure we are pushing ourselves to what we are fully capable of, but recurrent pain is far from a sign of progress; it is clearly a sign that you are doing something wrong and you need to look at your life with an objective lens.

## Amor Fati

Many ancient philosophers, such as Epictetus, and modern ones, such as Friedrich Nietzsche, wrote about the concept of Amor Fati, which is Latin for love fate. The concept behind it is to love whatever happens to you. Why love it? Because if you cannot change it then what is the point of hating it? The key is to keep your morale high and not be easily disgruntled as life takes turns that you did not expect it to take. There is something to be learned in everything that happens to us. There is something useful that can be extracted from every event that takes place in our lives. Remember, there is no good and bad with regards to what happens to you in life, only good and hidden good, so love it all. Love whatever happens because if you have to eat it, you might as well learn to enjoy it. You must learn to turn every bad into good. If you can't physically do that, then you must at least do it mentally by changing how you perceive it and thereafter how you feel about it.

# 22

# THE GIFT THAT KEEPS GIVING

*For it is in giving that we receive.*
— St. Francis of Assisi

It was a rainy evening in New York City. I could see from the window that it was the last hour of sunlight. All the work I had put in during the day seemed to have gone nowhere. Yet another day almost over and I was still so far from the results I was looking for with my new software company—no matter how much work I put in. So much hard work, so many team meetings, we'd tried so many different strategies, same result at the end. *Niente*. Nothing. Or at least that is how I saw it.

As the rain covered my window, I felt covered by my thoughts... Until they were interrupted by a phone call. Adam was calling me from overseas. My thoughts were completely preoccupied to take the call, but he knew of the big time difference and since I'd only met him once before, I figured it must be important for him. I decided to pick up out of politeness and make it a brief call. Adam is a super talented guy from the real estate industry. He is credited with being the creative and business genius behind one of the most charming beach towns in Florida. Adam built the town out of nothing, which he managed on behalf of a very wealthy billionaire.

My only encounter with Adam was earlier that year. I was meeting an acquaintance of mine, Henry, over dinner in Paris. I wanted to get to know Henry better to potentially recruit him to my software company, as he was in between jobs. Henry ended up bringing Adam with him to the dinner, as Adam was his ex-boss and friend. As I was getting introduced to Adam, Henry was trying to tell me a story about why he left his job when Adam cut him off halfway and bluntly said, "We both got pushed out." I was surprised in a good way with how frank Adam was, telling a stranger he just met that he basically got fired over a power struggle.

With that positive impression in mind, a few months later I coincidentally ran into a billionaire friend of mine while I was having coffee with someone from the old college days. He asked if he could crash our meeting and I joked that it wouldn't be the worst thing that he'd done. As we got to talking, he told me that his family just acquired one of the biggest companies in his industry in Europe and he was looking to recruit a lot of talent to help with the turnaround of this company along with other projects. Adam quickly came to mind. After we finished having coffee, I called Adam and asked him if he was interested and that I would be happy to make an introduction to my friend. Now it was Adam's turn to be surprised. He said he couldn't believe I would do such a nice thing for him after only meeting him once. He probably thanked me at least a dozen times on that call.

Now that I refreshed my memory with the only two interactions I'd had with Adam until that rainy day in New York, it made sense why he called me. He needed help. He tried knocking on so many doors that apparently seemed trustworthy but he kept getting disappointed; everyone was leaving him to hang dry. So I guess Adam was thinking, it doesn't hurt to try this guy Sherife who helped me unexpectedly before.

Apparently the billionaire that Adam used to work for was furious that Adam was not remorseful about leaving him and that, instead, Adam had a newfound success in the real estate industry after starting his own company. He was so bitter, especially about the fact that Adam was claiming unpaid compensation from commissions related to sales contracts that he was responsible for at the beach town. That billionaire decided to destroy Adam so that he remembered where he came from and would get down on his knees and kiss the king's ring and beg for mercy. To secure his plot, he got a few other billionaire friends involved who had contracts with Adam's new company. In little time, Adam found half a dozen lawsuits on his desk that were imploring him to pay hundreds of millions in damages.

It is no surprise that everyone left him hanging—who wants to cross swords with a gang of billionaires? For what upside? Adam? Everyone Adam knew already showed their hand. His friends, colleagues, people he'd helped in the past, nobody wanted any of this.

Just two minutes into our call in New York as he was spilling the beans on the deep pit he'd fallen into, I quickly realized how this was the last thing I needed in my day right then. I was just processing my own frustrations, my own pit that I couldn't seem to dig myself out of, that I only seemed to dig myself deeper and deeper into. There was no question that I did not have the time, the resources, or even the well-being to take on someone else's problems, let alone problems of this magnitude. It made complete sense to briefly communicate my sincere solidarity with what he was going through but that there was not much I could do, and even if I could, this was a really bad time. After all, even his closest friends didn't help him, so he wouldn't be surprised by this reaction from someone he'd only met once.

But that is not what happened. I probably spent two hours with Adam on the phone that day and many more hours as the weeks went by. Adam's biggest problem was that he couldn't think clearly. He was too blinded by the distress he was going through. He was being tortured emotionally, knowing who he was up against and that his most likely fate would be going to prison or ending up broke and cast out of the circles of elite society. His world came crashing quickly and so did his mental powers. He had very few people he could think with because everyone was being careful not to take the wrong side. Nobody wanted to make powerful enemies, especially if they felt there was no upside to the risk.

For me it was different. It was a matter of principle to start with. I don't recall I have ever turned down anyone that needed help before. I recall many times that the help people were asking me for was frustrating, underserved, or overreaching, but even in such circumstances, I never denied anyone help. At most I would limit the amount of help I would give, but I never slammed the door on someone in need, and so Adam was no different, even though he came with a very big price that would be paid by anyone who helped him. Apparently I wasn't just doing it to stay true to my nature. There was something far greater at work at a very deep and possibly invisible level that I wasn't aware of.

Every time I helped Adam, I felt great after. Here was a man who could offer me nothing, who had fallen from grace, who was covered in enough liability for anyone to stay as far away from him as possible. But every time I was having a really tough day at work and I hadn't heard from him in a while, I would call him, help him work out the latest problems he was facing in this saga, and my mood would turn around after. I would feel a relief, a renewed energy to give my own set of challenges another shot. I only realized this positive effect recently. I've helped hundreds of people like Adam in my life. He is probably the outlier with regards to the punishment I risked facing for helping him, but I could write volumes of books sharing the stories of all the people I've helped. Whether it was in a small or big way on my part, it always meant a lot to them.

It is very interesting how our biology is designed in a way to make us feel great, to do better when we help people. If only everyone realized this. It is not only a free way to feel great and be more productive but one that comes with the added bonus of making other people's lives great as well. If you don't believe it, try it yourself. Spend a week where you are mostly taking and spend another week where you are mostly giving. Then tell me which week felt better. You don't even need to have a professional core of skills that you can use to help people in that domain, although it is great if you do. Today the prevalent mentality has become every man for himself, so even the most basic form of emotional support will not go unnoticed in a world where very few people seem to care for anyone outside their personal lives, and the small circle of intimate people around them.

## Why do we feel better when we give?

Research studies that involve brain scans have shown that when we help people, it activates the same parts in the brain that responds to food and sex. Those endorphins that are released in your brain are considered "feel good" hormones. But such endorphins are only released when you are genuinely helping someone. The more time you give, the stronger the endorphin release. That is why it is better to give your time than to give just money. Depending on the cause, both could be important since the end result is how much of a difference you are making in someone's life.

## How to find people to help

You see them every day at work, in your family, in your close and extended circles of friends. Everyone needs help, but they don't show it because either people won't understand or they don't want to be perceived as weak and needy. Also, it is hard to notice if someone needs help when we are only looking at the surface. Try having deeper conversations with people. Ask them if they are having any challenges or if anything is giving them trouble. When they start talking, give them a chance to fully tell their story as opposed to just assuming and extrapolating what this is going to be about. In addition to your circle of people, there are plenty of orphanages, animal shelters, and children's hospitals that are always in need of visitors who are willing to share their humanity.

## How to help people

The effect of being heard out, knowing someone is listening to you attentively, that they care enough to be fully present with you—this is therapeutic in itself. People can feel significantly better from this simple practice alone, which, as simple as it is, does not come around very often. Most people get too caught up in sharing their opinion as opposed to fully listening to the person. If all you do is give people plenty of time to be heard, that alone is doing a lot. You can go beyond that as well by communicating that you feel what they are going through, and helping them reframe their self-image by telling them that it takes a very strong person to go through such things and still be standing on both feet. Give them credit.

When you feel that they have vented enough, you can start getting into the solution phase. Your job is not to give any recommendations or advice because you might not be in a position to do that. Your job is simply to help them structure their thinking properly, to identify the different options in front of them, to make them list the pros and cons of each option, to help them assess whether they are choosing an option for the right reasons, and to alert them to any dangers that they might not be aware of or highlight opportunities that they may have missed. It is for them to make the decision. Your role is to simply guide them into thinking about the situation in a rational and objective manner.

When you check on them every week, or every few weeks depending on the situation, they will report back any progress. You must find anything they did to commend them on, to motivate them, however small of a step they took. Find something you can encourage them about. If they went to see a psychologist, tell them how brave they are for taking that step. You can also share a story from your life that made you feel a similar way to how they are feeling now. It does not have to be the same situation, you just want to be vulnerable as well so that they can relate to you and it doesn't feel like you are looking down on them.

**What not to do when helping people**

Never blame them or tell them that the situation is their fault or call them stupid or judge them for what they did. Remember, you are trying to help people, not establish how much more intelligent you are. It is also important to watch out not to make them dependent on you. There might not be others who have been as caring to them as you have displayed and it is something they might start depending on you too much for. If you were to disappear for any reason it could hurt them. So it is best to make sure that you are always pushing them to get professional help, whether they need a doctor, a psychologist, or a lawyer, depending on the situation. Another reason for this is that it ensures you are not trying to provide any professional help. You are simply there to encourage them and to guide the process, not to provide services that you are not professionally qualified to do.

If you are wondering what happened with Adam, you'll be glad to know that he managed to fight back and clear himself of all of the lawsuits and that he is in a very happy and healthy place. Coincidently, I wrote this chapter on the eve of his birthday. I might find it challenging to count the number of times Adam thanks me any time he speaks to me or sees me. Seeing how big of a difference I made during this very difficult chapter of his life and keeping in mind how little effort it took on my part, it is a pity that we don't regularly make the difference we can in people's lives when the opportunity is always waiting at our fingertips.

*If you want happiness for an hour, take a nap.*
*If you want happiness for a day, go fishing. If you want*
*happiness for a year, inherit a fortune. If you want*
*happiness for a lifetime, help somebody.*
— Chinese Proverb

# 23

# LOOK FOR THE HIDDEN CUES

*Sometimes people don't want to hear the truth*
*because they don't want their illusions destroyed.*
— Friedrich Nietzsche

The Mediterranean. It was a nice summer day on the hotel rooftop pool. Southern Europe is always a great place to be in the summer. As that thought hit me, and I was taking in the summer breeze, three beautiful women walked past me and sat on the sun beds next to me. I was reading; I do not recall what I was reading at the time, but that is where my attention lay. Later on, one of them made an attempt to start a conversation with me. She pretended that she was not sure if I was talking to her or to someone else, so she looked at me and her friends and asked them if I was talking to her. The only problem with her approach was that I never actually said anything. I was silently reading my book.

So, out of politeness, I looked at her and smiled while I shook my head to indicate that I wasn't talking to her. She was wearing a very nice blue swimsuit.

After I was done reading I went for a swim and later came back to my sun bed to lay in the sun and get some color. As I was sitting down on my sun bed, I thought out of politeness I should speak to her, given her obvious attempt to start a conversation with me earlier when I was reading. I noticed she was having lunch, so I simply asked her, "How is the food here?" "Not bad," she responded, and then she didn't stop speaking for the next thirty minutes.

Apparently she and her friends were famous actresses from different countries. She had a very bubbly personality, very expressive facial features, and she was quite opinionated, that is why she didn't stop talking, but she was very entertaining. Although I enjoyed the conversation, I had enough being polite, so I picked up my notebook and started writing. She asked me if I was playing crosswords, I smiled and said, "No, I'm writing." She asked me if I was a writer. It seemed there was no getting away from her. I smiled and said, "I am trying to be..." I meant that I was trying to write in that moment, despite her interruptions, but also that I was actually working on launching a career in writing as I was working on my first book. She kept the conversation going regardless.

As the sun set and the rooftop pool was closing, she indicated that she would be going to a beach in Latin America where I was planning to be as well in a few weeks. I was thinking that I didn't know a lot of people there, so some additional company would not hurt, so I asked her to message me when she got there. She proceeded to take my contact info and we connected on social media. That is when I realized they were famous in their respective countries, given the large number of followers they had and their verified accounts. Apparently we were also staying at the same hotel.

A couple of days later, she messaged me asking what I was doing the following day. I told her I had plans but we could meet the day after. She said that tomorrow was her last day. As much as I would have liked to get to know her better, I had already decided that I wanted to take the day to myself, so I said I was sure we would meet again in the future.

A few weeks later she commented on one of my posts on social media, saying that we were in the same city and that we should meet up! We made plans for lunch. We spent a few hours where I really got to know her. I found it interesting how expressive she was. She could really talk for hours on all sorts of topics, and she was full of intellect and well traveled. She also wasn't just a yes-woman; she challenged me on a number of my opinions in the conversation. I started to like her. When the bill came, she said she would be happy to split, and I said, next time. She smiled and said thanks.

The next day we started messaging. The energy in her voice messages reflected her personality so well, which I liked. She was like an Energizer bunny, the way she spoke. I started to like her more. I seemed to have hit a chord with her. Then on the third day after our first lunch, out of nowhere she asked if I wanted to meet her the next day because she was traveling the day after. That was bold. But I like bold women. It was actually a turn-on. So I made plans for lunch.

Between the time we were messaging to make plans and the first ten minutes of our lunch, I noticed a few red flags. But I overlooked them. After all, she was the one that asked me out and really wanted to see me before she traveled. She put herself on the spot. At the end of our meal, as the waiter placed the bill in the middle of the table, she said that she had to pay something this time. I grabbed the bill and asked the waiter to bring the credit card machine. She said, "You are not going to let me pay anything, are you?" I gave the waiter my credit card and he processed the payment.

So what impression did you form of her when it came to finances? Was she someone who was financially independent? Did she expect men to pay for her meals? Did she have a romantic interest in me?

Something was not sitting well with me after that lunch. I could not put my finger on it, but something was off, although everything seemed fine at the surface. So, I replayed the day in my mind and noticed every single subtle reaction, or the lack of one. I then slept on it, and when I woke up, I decided I wouldn't see her again. Despite the fact that she liked me and enjoyed my company, it was clear to me that she just wanted interesting company who would provide for her as well—a sponsor of some sort. Although, she made every effort to give a different impression. She was not in love with me. What gave her away?

While I chose a romantic story to demonstrate the lesson in this chapter, this is actually a life lesson, not just a romantic lesson. You can apply it at work, with friends, and in all areas of your life. The lesson here is that you need to focus your attention not just on the things that happen, but more importantly on the things that don't happen. We easily get carried away in the things that happen. It becomes difficult to look for or notice the things that did not happen. In the story above, what gave her away is that although she offered to pay three times, she did not reach for her purse a single time. There is a big difference between actually wanting to pay and wanting to come across as someone who is willing to pay. The first person will make a physical effort to pay by grabbing the bill or reaching out for their wallet. They will sometimes even play a tug of war over the physical bill. The second will find it enough to use words. My point here is not who is supposed to pay for lunch. My point is how to catch someone that is only pretending.

That is the first step in this framework: to notice the things that did not happen. That is how Sherlock Holmes solved a major crime in Arthur Doyle's story *Silver Blaze*. He solved the crime by noting that the family dog had not barked during the murder, which made him realize that the murderer must have been someone that the dog knew. This immediately reduced the number of suspects from an open ended list to only a few. We rarely pay attention to what should have happened but did not happen because it is our natural tendency to focus on positive information and get carried away in it. Instead, we must learn to visualize the absence of something as easily as we see the presence of something.

After we notice something missing, the second step is to play back the whole film, looking for other cues or red flags that might have been too subtle to notice the first time, cues that now stand out when we look back, after we have been tipped off by what was missing. You might be thinking that I jumped to conclusions too quickly, maybe even that I was too harsh in my judgment of her. But I only came to that conclusion when I rewinded everything that happened between us since our first encounter. It was then that I noticed many red flags that were too subtle to notice earlier. I only came to my conclusion after I connected all the dots, after I played back the film several times. That last bill incident only tipped me off to do a playback review; I did not jump to a conclusion when the bill came.

Oftentimes, when we are on course to getting something we want or doing something we enjoy we tend to overlook what seems to be minor interruptions that don't fit with the big picture. It is a form of wishful thinking. While we should not go to the other extreme and abort any plans we are pursuing because of the slightest red flag, there is a middle ground that is necessary. That middle ground involves noticing any minor events that don't fit into the overall expected behavior and keeping those events in a mental waiting room as opposed to giving excuses for those red flags. As additional minor red flags play out, one must go back to the waiting room and analyze those together. When those little things add up, they become a giant that stares you in the face.

In summary, don't just get carried away in the positive things that happen. Notice the things that did not happen. Once you notice something that did not happen, do a playback for the whole encounter, looking at it with fresh eyes. Spot any other events that seem out of place and could connect with what triggered the review process to form a new theory or explanation. It helps to discuss the event with someone you trust. There is a benefit to saying it out loud. It is also good to get a good night's sleep after that discussion to give your brain the chance to process everything. You will be able to see better the next day.

# 24

## TAKE A BREAK FROM THE BATTLEFIELD

*The wise man does at once what the fool does finally.*
— Niccolo Machiavelli

There was a time when people finished work at four o'clock. Once they left the office, they left their work behind. Weekends were rarely interrupted by work unless there was an emergency. Emergencies rarely happened. People had plenty of time to relax and recharge their batteries; they were ready for a fresh start for the next day or week of work. That time is long gone. Managers are more demanding than ever when it comes to their employees. Advanced communication tools such as smart phones and emails have extended work hours after employees leave the office, into their homes and bedrooms. Weekends have become unofficial part-time workdays and vacations are never full vacations anymore due to the connectivity to work that still remains through smart phones.

At the same time, the prominence of social media and our addiction to our smartphones and digital media consumption have resulted in our constant engagement by these throughout the day. It has become a rare sight for someone to be able to regularly relax and reflect for a full hour without their attention being broken by a phone notification or their urge to check their phone. The result is that we now live in a constant, never-ending marathon. Our batteries have been drained, our brain has been reconditioned, and its reward circuits manipulated. It is part of the reason why we are not as happy, feel constantly fatigued, and are sometimes not sure of where we are going.

This hyper-marathon that the whole world seems to be on makes it difficult for most people who even realize the need to take a step back. Because they would instantly stand out as taking a step back, their colleagues might look at them like they are not engaged in their work, they are too slow to respond to emails, they leave the office early, etc. So this shame culture and the fear of being harassed by the rest of the pack is sometimes why some people choose to continue being drained to avoid being cast out by their colleagues.

## Stop

In a society that urges mindless moving forward, we have forgotten the crucial roles that sleep and rest play in our lives. They are not activities reserved for lazy people. There is a reason why elite athletes insist on getting at least eight hours of sleep every night. Do you know where muscles grow? Not in the gym, in SWS. SWS stands for slow-wave sleep, a sleep cycle also known as deep sleep. Deep sleep is when your body repairs any broken tissue and grows muscle. Without getting enough sleep, you completely limit your physical gains. Do you know where new lessons learned are processed in your memory? Not in the classroom, in REM. That is another sleep cycle that stands for rapid eye movement. If you don't get enough sleep, it's difficult to retain the full lessons that you worked very hard to learn. The quality and quantity of your sleep determine the duration you spend in the different types of sleep cycles that you go through—SWS, REM, light sleep, etc.

I hope this makes you completely rethink the priority that sleep should take in your life. For most people it has become the first thing we cut down on when we are short on time. We sleep whatever hours are left in the day after we have done everything else. I used to be like that. In college we used to brag about only getting three or four hours of sleep. I completely changed since I learned about the importance of sleep. Now, I cancel certain things in my day because I realize it will seriously infringe on my sleep. If I infringe on my sleep, I will also infringe on my performance and mood. Not getting enough sleep for one day because something urgent came up is OK. What is not OK is for cutting back on sleep to be the norm. Keep in mind that there is something called sleep debt, where your body keeps track of the hours of sleep it needed and it did not get. Your body expects you to pay off your sleep debt by sleeping more on future nights to make up for sleeping less on the nights before.

Similar to sleep is the concept of rest. Rest is not the same thing as watching TV on the couch or scrolling through social media on your phone. Both of these activities still require your brain to be engaged. When you make time for complete rest throughout the day, when you are not keeping your brain busy with senseless activities, you give time for your brain to create magic. Inspiration, epiphanies, *aha* moments, these are things that come when your brain has been given time to connect the dots and spot patterns it has been coming across. Why do you think some of the best writers and artists in history lived a bohemian lifestyle where they needed to sink their senses in nature, overlooking the sea, gazing at the stars. It was the free time their brain needed in order to respond with a rush of ideas never seen before. Harness the same power these legendary artists had by giving yourself the full downtime you need throughout the day, time for yourself alone, time for your brain to produce what it wants without having to do things that you demand it to do.

## Halftime

When it comes to professional sports, why are games organized with at least one halftime in between, depending on the sport? No, it is not because the players get tired; they are elite athletes who could play a full game without a break if they had to. The real benefit of the halftime is an extremely valuable opportunity to get off the court and take a few minutes to think about the big picture. How did it go relative to the plan? What went wrong? What changes need to be made? Courtesy of this halftime, players can get back to the game with a renewed focus on their goals, a clear awareness of their mistakes and the distractions that might have occurred in the first half, along with a new strategy that deals with the surprises that took place.

How much more complicated are our lives relative to a sports game? Don't we need the same halftime? Athletes don't take halftime because they are lazy, so why do we shame ourselves when we think about taking extra time off? We need to rethink the big picture, to reassess if we are still the same person we were when we first embarked on that new job, career, or project. To think about whether the goal we are working on still suits us in the first place. Even if we rationally decide that we are still in the right place, are we pursuing the right strategy? Has time demonstrated that this is the right team? Are we moving at the right pace? For the same reasons elite athletes need to get off the court when assessing these questions, so do we. It is why kings sometimes order a truce when waging war in order to ask the same questions about the battles that are underway.

When you are in the middle of the battlefield, your adrenaline is running at its peak, your emotions are fully stimulated. It is hard to be rational and fully objective in such an environment. You are much more likely to continue the course if you were to think about making changes when you are in the middle of the action. When you are a warrior in full force, you don't even notice your cuts and wounds, you don't feel the blood spilling. It is only during the truce that you notice the true depth of your wounds, when you notice how sore your muscles actually feel.

Take time off—a week, a month, or even a year. Don't wait until you burn out. The time you need to recover and repair from burnout could be dramatically reduced had you stopped just a few weeks before fully burning out. It is like a car that's running on an empty tank. Time off is not just for people who are tired, it is for people who don't want to fall victim to their delusions, who want to be refreshed with new ideas and ways of thinking. Do it in the way that works best for you. Whether in the form of small chunks of time off through the year or a bigger time off. The important point is that you do it . . . before you burn out.

Sometimes slowing down is the best way to charge ahead.

# FINALE

*Success is going from failure to*
*failure without losing enthusiasm.*
— Winston Churchill

When life seems to be going against you. When you feel stuck. When it becomes difficult to make meaning out of your challenges and misfortunes. When it seems the world is out to get you. When you feel like you are being treated unfairly. It is easy to feel helpless in these situations and to contemplate giving up. Sometimes people seek some form of revenge against the world, and subscribing to radical ideas that blame some segment of society for our collective misfortunes can become an outlet. Others take refuge in momentary pleasure, as a form of distraction, as a way to numb the pain. But the pain seems to still be there the next morning, which can create a cyclical relationship with temporary pleasure that can lead to some form of addiction.

Instead of blaming the world, you must look inward for the answers. Could this have been avoided? Not necessarily the last step. But if you go ten steps back, did you have other options then? Possibly. Would they have led elsewhere? Certainly. Every move you make in life unleashes a domino effect. It's easy to go off track, but that doesn't make you a bad person, just someone that wasn't alert enough or conscious of their shortcomings. Many times we feel that we know what we are doing when in reality we are clueless. That realization can take many years to sink in.

We do not go through one phase of childhood. We go through many. Different parts of our characters continue to grow, parts still undeveloped even during adulthood. Whenever you find yourself feeling that you have failed in a colossal way, whether it is in your personal or professional life, that is you having gone through another childhood development phase. But to fully mature out of this phase, you need to fully digest and synthesize the lessons learned and the causes that led to this outcome. You will almost always initially be inclined to cast blame on the outside world. The more you do that, the longer you simply delay the recovery process.

It takes courage, intelligence, and maturity to look inside for the mistakes, shortcomings, and shortsightedness that might have led to your situation. There are usually several mistakes lurking below your radar. They could even be disguised as strengths, things you were proud of, that you may eventually realize are weaknesses or liabilities. So, was it something you did, was it a series of actions that needed to be rectified, or was it a problem with your perception, of how you saw events, people, your actions, and how you saw your very own self. Was there anything at all related to your actions or thinking (or lack of actions or lack of thinking) that could be linked to the situation you find yourself in?

OK, now you begin to find some suspects, but you say that it isn't enough to deserve what happened to you. Deserve? That is irrelevant. Life and nature are governed by laws and forces. When a teacup is dropped from a balcony, it is pulled to the ground and smashed to pieces by the force of gravity. Did the teacup deserve this? It is not a question whether you deserve it or not, life does not operate that way. It is a question of whether your actions and your thoughts could have led to this situation. Even if you didn't deserve it.

Once you realize that, you should be relieved. Because if your misfortunes can be traced back to you, then you can do something to reverse them. It would be a much more helpless situation if life was just randomly picking on you. Pick up yourself, find your shortcomings, overcome this phase of learning. You have many more lives inside you that are yet to be unleashed. Don't settle for a life of victimhood and pointing fingers. It's time to get up again. It's time to look inside. It's time to build your Super Vision.

# ACKNOWLEDGMENTS

*If I have seen further,*
*it is by standing on the shoulders of giants.*
— Sir Isaac Newton

It is very hard to write something that has never been written before, given the vast number of books that have been available for thousands of years on a diverse number of topics. I have recently rediscovered the importance of reading books regularly and the potent knowledge sitting idle in many books, waiting to transform our minds and our lives once we pick them up and make their wisdom an intrinsic part of our lifestyle. I am so grateful for the many writers who came before me and so humbled that now I have a craft in common with them. Something that is more than a profession, a calling to share insights that must not remain with us, that must not die with us, but must be shared with all of mankind so that they may unleash the powerful transformation that awaits them. I will forever remain a student to all of those who wrote before me. It can be an adventure to discover a new teacher, given there are so many waiting to cross paths with you when you discover them in a library or bookstore.

I want to thank Yousriya Sawiris. I would not have written this book if she was not so relentless in pushing me. I would also like to thank my friend Nahla for all the times we made fun of each other that never cease to put a smile on my face and has ultimately become our very own coping mechanism. Humor is far more than the best medicine. You can never run out of it and it is free. From time to time, she will manage to say something serious that is also useful. She was the first person to recognize that my personal stories and my unique voice will be the most special mark about my writing.

It would have been much harder to write and publish this book if it wasn't for the recent wave of technological progress that has shaken the book industry, for which I am grateful. It is easy to downplay the effort it took to navigate this new industry and quickly get a grip of the best practices to apply and build a great team. I am thankful for my entrepreneurial background for helping me navigate this process. Even after I decided to take off the business suit, it still finds its way back into my life.

Last but not least, I want to thank my heavenly father, who has made us in his own image. I know I put you through a lot of trouble. But you knew it was going to happen when you made me. Thank you for your patience and your love.

# NEWSLETTER

If you enjoyed reading this book and would like to get similar insights from me on a regular basis, you can join my mailing list. Simply send an email to mr.wellbeing@icloud.com with the word "Newsletter" in the subject line and you will be subscribed to my newsletter.

Let's stay in touch,
Sherife

Printed in Great Britain
by Amazon

30109546R10126